Marx Joyce
Abbott Hardy Montaigne Machiavelli Chesterton Cooper Emerson Austen
Defoe Melville Haggard Hugo
Christie Eliot Grimm
Stoker Carroll Molière
Wilde Maupassant Byron
Fitzgerald Einstein Engels Schiller
Garnett Smith
Goethe Hawthorne Kafka
Dostoyevsky Hall
Cotton
Baum Kipling Doyle Willis
Leslie Dumas Henry Nietzsche
Flaubert Turgenev Balzac
Stockton Vatsyayana Crane
Burroughs Verne
Curtis Tocqueville Whitman Gogol Vinci
Homer Widger Tolstoy Busch
Darwin Thoreau
Potter Freud Zola Lawrence Twain Plato Scott
Kant Jowett Stevenson Dickens
Andersen Burton Hesse Harte
London Descartes Cervantes
Poe Aristotle Wells Voltaire
Hale James Hastings
Bunner Shakespeare Cooke
Richter Chambers Irving
Chekhov da
Doré Swift Dante Shaw Wodehouse Benedict Alcott
Pushkin
Newton

tredition®

tredition was established in 2006 by Sandra Latusseck and Soenke Schulz. Based in Hamburg, Germany, tredition offers publishing solutions to authors and publishing houses, combined with worldwide distribution of printed and digital book content. tredition is uniquely positioned to enable authors and publishing houses to create books on their own terms and without conventional manufacturing risks.

For more information please visit: www.tredition.com

TREDITION CLASSICS

This book is part of the TREDITION CLASSICS series. The creators of this series are united by passion for literature and driven by the intention of making all public domain books available in printed format again - worldwide. Most TREDITION CLASSICS titles have been out of print and off the bookstore shelves for decades. At tredition we believe that a great book never goes out of style and that its value is eternal. Several mostly non-profit literature projects provide content to tredition. To support their good work, tredition donates a portion of the proceeds from each sold copy. As a reader of a TREDITION CLASSICS book, you support our mission to save many of the amazing works of world literature from oblivion. See all available books at www.tredition.com.

Project Gutenberg

The content for this book has been graciously provided by Project Gutenberg. Project Gutenberg is a non-profit organization founded by Michael Hart in 1971 at the University of Illinois. The mission of Project Gutenberg is simple: To encourage the creation and distribution of eBooks. Project Gutenberg is the first and largest collection of public domain eBooks.

The Witchcraft Delusion in Colonial Connecticut (1647-1697)

John Metcalf Taylor

Imprint

This book is part of TREDITION CLASSICS

Author: John Metcalf Taylor
Cover design: Buchgut, Berlin – Germany

Publisher: tredition GmbH, Hamburg - Germany
ISBN: 978-3-8424-5061-5

www.tredition.com
www.tredition.de

[Illustration: A Grand Jury Presentment for Witchcraft Reproduced from the original in the Connecticut Historical Society, Hartford

May it please yr Honble Court, we the Grand inquest now setting for the County of Fairefeild, being made sensable, not only by Common fame (but by testamonies duly billed to us) that the widow Mary Staple, Mary Harvey ye wife of Josiah Harvey & Hannah Harvey the daughter of the saide Josiah, all of Fairefeild, remain under the susspition of useing witchecraft, which is abomanable both in ye sight of God & man and ought to bc witnessed against. we doe therefore (in complyance to our duty, the discharge of our oathes and that trust reposed in us) presente the above mentioned pssons to the Honble Court of Assistants now setting in Fairefeild, that they may be taken in to Custody & proceeded against according to their demerits.

Fairefeild, Fby, 1692 in behalfe of the Grnd Jury JOSEPH BASTARD, foreman]

THE WITCHCRAFT DELUSION IN COLONIAL CONNECTICUT

1647-1697

BY JOHN M. TAYLOR

Author of "Maximilian and Carlotta, a Story of Imperialism," and "Roger Ludlow, the Colonial Lawmaker"

REPRINTED 1974 BY CORNER HOUSE PUBLISHERS

"Connecticut can well afford to
let her records go to the world."
Blue Laws: True and False (p. 47).
J. HAMMOND TRUMBULL.

FOREWORD

The true story of witchcraft in old Connecticut has never been told. It has been hidden in the ancient records and in manuscripts in private collections, and those most conversant with the facts have not made them known, for one reason or another. It is herein written from authoritative sources, and should prove of interest and value as a present-day interpretation of that strange delusion, which for a half century darkened the lives of the forefathers and foremothers of the colonial days.

J.M.T.
Hartford, Connecticut.

TWO INDICTMENTS FOR WITCHCRAFT

"John Carrington thou art indited by the name of John Carrington of Wethersfield—carpenter—, that not hauing the feare of God before thine eyes thou hast interteined ffamilliarity with Sattan the great enemye of God and mankinde and by his helpe hast done workes aboue the course of nature for wch both according to the lawe of God and the established lawe of this Commonwealth thou deseruest to dye."

Record Particular Court, 2: 17, 1650-51.

"Hugh Crotia, Thou Standest here presented by the name of Hugh Crotia of Stratford in the Colony of Connecticut in New England; for that not haueing the fear of God before thine Eyes, through the Instigation of the Devill, thou hast forsaken thy God & covenanted with the Devill, and by his help hast in a preternaturall way afflicted the bodys of Sundry of his Majesties good Subjects, for which according to the Law of God, and the Law of this Colony, thou deseruest to dye."

Record Court of Assistants, 2: 16, 1693.

A WARRANT FOR THE EXECUTION OF A WITCH [A] AND THE SHERIFF'S RETURN THEREON

To George Corwin Gentlm high Sheriff of the County of Essex Greeting

Whereas Bridgett Bishop als Olliver the wife of Edward Bishop of Salem in the County of Essex Sawyer at a special Court of Oyer and Terminer ---- (held at?) [B] Salem this second Day of this instant month of June for the Countyes of Essex Middlesex and Suffolk before William Stoughton Esqe. and his Associates Justices of the said Court was Indicted and arraigned upon five several Indictments for useing practising & exercising on the ---- [B] last past and divers others days ---- [B] witchcraft in and upon the bodyes of Abigail Williams Ann puttnam Jr Mercy Lewis Mary Walcott and Elizabeth Hubbard of Salem Village single women; whereby their bodyes were hurt afflicted pined consumed wasted & tormented contrary to the forme of the statute in that case made and provided To which Indictmts the said Bridgett Bishop pleaded not guilty and for Tryall thereof put herselfe upon God and her Country ---- [B] she was found guilty of the ffelonyes and Witchcrafts whereof she stood Indicted and sentence of death accordingly passed agt her as the Law directs execution whereof yet remaines to be done These are therefore in the name of their Majties William & Mary now King & Queen over England & to will and command you that upon Fryday next being the fourth day of this instant month of June between the hours of Eight and twelve in the aforenoon of the same day you safely conduct the sd Bridgett Bishop als Olliver from their Majties Goale in Salem aforesd to the place of execution and there cause her to be hanged by the neck until she be dead and of your doings herein make returne to the Clerk of the sd Court and precept And hereof you are not to faile at your peril And this shall be sufficient warrant Given under my hand & seal at Boston the Eighth of June in the ffourth year of the reigne of our Sovereigne Lords William & Mary now King & Queen over England Annoque Dm 1692 Wm. Stoughton

[A] Original in office of Clerk of the Courts at Salem, Massachusetts. Said to be the only one extant in American archives.

[B] Some of the words in the warrant are illegible.

June 16 1692

According to the within written precept I have taken the Bodye of the within named Bridgett Bishop out of their Majties Goale in Salem & Safely Conueighd her to the place provided for her Execution & Caused ye sd Bridgett to be hanged by the neck till Shee was dead all which was according to the time within Required & So I make returne by me George Corwin Sheriff

CONTENTS

CHAPTER I Perkins' definition—Burr's "Servants of Satan"—The monkish idea—The ancientness of witchcraft—Its universality—Its regulation—What it was—Its oldest record—The Babylonian Stele—Its discovery—King Hammurabi's Code, 2250 B.C.—Its character and importance—Hebraic resemblances—Its witchcraft law—The test of guilt—The water test. . . . 1-5

CHAPTER II Opinions of Blackstone and Lecky—Witchcraft nomenclature—Its earlier and later phases—Common superstitions—Monna Sidonia's invocation—Leland's Sea Song—Witchcraft's diverse literature—Its untold history— The modern Satanic idea—Exploitation by the Inquisitors—The chief authorities—The witch belief—Its recognition in drama and romance—The Weird Sisters—Other characters. . . . 6-14

CHAPTER III Fundamentals—The scriptural citations—Old and New Testament—Josephus—Ancient and modern witchcraft—The distinction—The arch enemy Satan—Action of the Church—The later definition—The New England indictments—Satan's recognition—Persecutions in Italy, Germany and France—Slow spread to England—Statute of Henry VIII—Cranmer's injunction—Jewell's sermon—Statute James I—His Demonologie—Executions in Eastern England—Witch finder Hopkins—Howell's statement—John Lowes—Witchcraft in Scotland—Commissions—Instruments of torture—Forbes' definition—Colonial beliefs. . . . 15-22

CHAPTER IV Fiske's view—The forefathers' belief—Massachusetts, Connecticut and New Haven laws—Sporadic cases—The Salem tragedy—Statements of Hawthorne, Fiske, Lowell, Latimer—The victims—Upham's picture—The trial court—Sewall's confession—Cotton Mather—Calef and Upham—Poole—Mather's rules—Ministerial counsel—Longfellow's opinion—Mather's responsibility—His own evidence—Conspectus. . . . 23-34

CHAPTER V The Epidemic in Connecticut—Palfrey—Trumbulls—Winthrop's Journal—Treatment of witchcraft—Silence and evasion—The true story—How told—Witnesses—Testimony—All classes affected—The courts—Judges and jurors—The best evidence—The record—Grounds for examination of a witch—Jones' summary—Witch marks—What they were—How discovered—Dalton's Country Justice—The searchers—Searchers' report in Disborough and Clawson cases. . . . 35-44

CHAPTER VI Hamersley's and Morgan's comment—John Allyn's letter—The accusation—Its origin—Its victims—Many witnesses—Record evidence—The witnesses themselves—Memorials of their delusion—Notable depositions—Selected testimonies, and cases—Katherine Harrison—The court—The judge—The indictment—Grand jury's oath—Credulity of the court—Testimony—Its unique character—Bracy—Dickinson—Montague— Graves—Francis—Johnson—Hale—Smith—Verdict and sentence—Court's appeal to the ministers—Their answer—A remarkable document—Katherine's petition—"A Complaint of severall grieuances"—Katherine's reprieve— Dismissal from imprisonment—Removal. . . . 45-61

CHAPTER VII Mercy Disborough—Cases at Fairfield, 1692—The special court—The indictment—Testimonies—Jesop—Barlow—Dunning—Halliberch—Benit— Grey—Godfree—Search for witch marks—Ordeal by water Cateran Branch's accusation—Jury disagree—Later verdict of guilty—The governor's sentence—Reference to General Court—Afterthought—John Hale's conclusion—Courts call on the ministers—Their answer—General advice—Reasons for reprieve—Notable papers—Eliot and Woodbridge—Willis—Pitkin—Stanly—The pardon. . . . 62-78

CHAPTER VIII Hawthorne—Latimer—Additional cases—Curious and vulgar testimony—All illustrative of opinion—Make it understandable—Elizabeth Seager—Witnesses—What they swore to—Garretts—Sterne—Hart—Willard— Pratt—Migat—"Staggerings" of the jury—Contradictions—Verdict— Elizabeth Godman—Governor Goodyear's dilemma—Strange doings—Ball's information—Imprisonment—Discharge—Nathaniel and Rebecca Greensmith— Character, Accusation—Rebecca's confession—Conviction—Double execution at Hartford. . . . 79-100

CHAPTER IX Elizabeth Clawson—The indictment—Witnesses—"Kateran" Branch—Garney— Kecham—Abigail and Nathaniel Cross—Bates—Sargent Wescot and Abigail— Finch—Bishop—Holly—Penoir—Slawson—Kateran's Antics—Acquittal. Hugh Crotia—The court—Grand jury—Indictment—Testimony—Confession— Acquittal—Gaol delivery—Elizabeth Garlick—A sick woman's fancies—"A black thing at the bed's featte"—Burning herbs—The sick child—The ox' broken leg—The dead ram and sow—The Tale burning. . . . 101-121

CHAPTER X Goodwife Knapp—Her character—A notable case—Imprisonment—Harsh treatment—The inquisitors—Their urgency—Knapp's appeal—The postmortem desecration—Prominent people involved—Davenport and Ludlow—Staplies vs. Ludlow—The court—Confidential gossip—Cause of the suit—Testimony—Davenport—Sherwood—Tomson—Gould—Ward—Pell—Brewster—Lockwood—Hull— Brundish—Whitlock—Barlow—Lyon—Mistress Staplies—Her doings aforetime— Tashs' night ride—"A light woman"—Her character—Reparation suit—Her later indictment—Power of the delusion—Pertinent inquiry. . . . 122-141

CHAPTER XI Present opinions—J. Hammond Trumbull—Annie Eliot Trumbull—Review—Authenticity—Record evidence—Controversialists—Actual cases—Suspicions—Accusations—Acquittals—Flights—Executions—First complete roll—Changes in belief—Contrast—Edwards—Carter—"The Rogerenes"—Conclusion—Hathorne—Mather. . . . 142-160

THE WITCHCRAFT DELUSION IN COLONIAL CONNECTICUT

CHAPTER I

"First, because Witchcraft is a rife and common sinne in these our daies, and very many are intangled with it, beeing either practitioners thereof in their owne persons, or at the least, yielding to seeke for helpe and counsell of such as practise it." *A Discovrse of the Damned Art of Witchcraft,* PERKINS, 1610.

"And just as God has his human servants, his church on earth, so also the Devil has his—men and women sworn to his service and true to his bidding. To win such followers he can appear to men in any form he pleases, can deceive them, enter into compact with them, initiate them into his worship, make them his allies for the ruin of their fellows. Now it is these human allies and servants of Satan, thus postulated into existence by the brain of a monkish logician, whom history knows as witches." *The Literature of Witchcraft,* BURR.

Witchcraft in its generic sense is as old as human history. It has written its name in the oldest of human records. In all ages and among all peoples it has taken firm hold on the fears, convictions and consciences of men. Anchored in credulity and superstition, in the dread and love of mystery, in the hard and fast theologic doctrines and teachings of diabolism, and under the ban of the law from its beginning, it has borne a baleful fruitage in the lives of the learned and the unlearned, the wise and the simple.

King and prophet, prelate and priest, jurist and lawmaker, prince and peasant, scholars and men of affairs have felt and dreaded its subtle power, and sought relief in code and commandment, bull and anathema, decree and statute—entailing even the penalty of death—and all in vain until in the march of the races to a higher civilization, the centuries enthroned faith in the place of fear, wisdom in the place of ignorance, and sanity in the seat of delusion.

In its earlier historic conception witchcraft and its demonstrations centered in the claim of power to produce certain effects, "things beyond the course of nature," from supernatural causes, and under this general term all its occult manifestations were classified with magic and sorcery, until the time came when the Devil was identified and acknowledged both in church and state as the originator and sponsor of the mystery, sin and crime—the sole father of the Satanic compacts with men and women, and the law both canonical and civil took cognizance of his malevolent activities.

In the Acropolis mound at Susa in ancient Elam, in the winter of 1901-2, there was brought to light by the French expedition in charge of the eminent savant, M. de Morgan, one of the most remarkable memorials of early civilization ever recovered from the buried cities of the Orient.

It is a monolith—a stele of black diorite—bearing in bas-relief a likeness of Hammurabi (the Amrephel of the Old Testament; Genesis xiv, 1), and the sixth king of the first Babylonian dynasty, who reigned about 2250 B.C.; and there is also carved upon it, in archaic script in black letter cuneiform—used long after the cursive writing was invented—the longest Babylonian record discovered to this day,—the oldest body of laws in existence and the basis of historical jurisprudence.

It is a remarkable code, quickly made available through translation and transliteration by the Assyrian scholars, and justly named, from its royal compiler, Hammurabi's code. He was an imperialist in purpose and action, and in the last of his reign of fifty-five years he annexed or assimilated the suzerainty of Elam, or Southern Persia, with Assyria to the north, and also Syria and Palestine, to the Mediterranean Sea.

This record in stone originally contained nineteen columns of inscriptions of four thousand three hundred and fourteen lines, arranged in two hundred and eighty sections, covering about two hundred separate decisions or edicts. There is substantial evidence that many of the laws were of greater antiquity than the code itself, which is a thousand years older than the Mosaic code, and there are many striking resemblances and parallels between its provisions, and the law of the covenant, and the deuteronomy laws of the Hebrews.

The code was based on personal responsibility. It protects the sanctity of an oath before God, provides among many other things for written evidence in legal matters, and is wonderfully comprehensive and rich in rules for the conduct of commercial, civic, financial, social, economic, and domestic affairs.

These sections are notably illustrative:

"If a man, in a case (pending judgment), utters threats against the witnesses (or), does not establish the testimony that he has given, if that case be a case involving life, that man shall be put to death.

"If a judge pronounces a judgment, renders a decision, delivers a verdict duly signed and sealed and afterwards alters his judgment, they shall call that judge to account for the alteration of the judgment which he had pronounced, and he shall pay twelvefold the penalty which was in the said judgment, and, in the assembly, they shall expel him from his seat of judgment, and he shall not return, and with the judges in a case he shall not take his seat.

"If a man practices brigandage and is captured, that man shall be put to death.

"If a woman hates her husband, and says: 'thou shalt not have me,' they shall inquire into her antecedents for her defects; and if she has been a careful mistress and is without reproach and her husband has been going about and greatly belittling her, that woman has no blame. She shall receive her presents and shall go to her father's house.

"If she has not been a careful mistress, has gadded about, has neglected her house and has belittled her husband, they shall throw that woman into the water.

"If a physician operates on a man for a severe wound with a bronze lancet and causes the man's death, or opens an abscess (in the eye) of a man with a bronze lancet and destroys the man's eye, they shall cut off his fingers.

"If a builder builds a house for a man and does not make its construction firm and the house, which he has built, collapses and causes the death of the owner of the house, that builder shall be put to death."

It is, however, with only one of King Hammurabi's wise laws that this inquiry has to do, and it is this:

"If a man has placed an enchantment upon a man, and has not justified himself, he upon whom the enchantment is placed to the Holy River (Euphrates) shall go; into the Holy River he shall plunge. If the Holy River holds (drowns) him he who enchanted him shall take his house. If on the contrary, the man is safe and thus is innocent, the wizard loses his life, and his house."

Or, as another translation has it:

"If a man ban a man and cast a spell on him—if he cannot justify it he who has banned shall be killed."

"If a man has cast a spell on a man and has not justified it, he on whom the spell has been thrown shall go to the River God, and plunge into the river. If the River God takes him he who has banned him shall be saved. If the River God show him to be innocent, and he be saved, he who banned him shall be killed, and he who plunged into the river shall take the house of him who banned him."

There can be no more convincing evidence of the presence and power of the great witchcraft superstition among the primitive races than this earliest law; and it is to be especially noted that it prescribes one of the very tests of guilt—the proof by water—which was used in another form centuries later, on the continent, in England and New England, at Wurzburg and Bonn, at Rouen, in Suffolk, Essex and Devon, and at Salem and Hartford and Fairfield, when "the Devil starteth himself up in the pulpit, like a meikle black man, and calling the row (roll) everyone answered, Here!"

CHAPTER II

"To deny the possibility, nay actual evidence of witchcraft and sorcery, is at once to flatly contradict the revealed word of God in various passages both of the Old and New Testaments." *Blackstone's Commentaries* (Vol. 4, ch. 4, p. 60).

"It was simply the natural result of Puritanical teaching acting on the mind, predisposing men to see Satanic influence in life, and consequently eliciting the phenomena of witchcraft." LECKY's *Rationalism in Europe* (Vol. I, p. 123).

Witchcraft's reign in many lands and among many peoples is also attested in its remarkable nomenclature. Consider its range in ancient, medieval and modern thought as shown in some of its definitions: Magic, sorcery, soothsaying, necromancy, astrology, wizardry, mysticism, occultism, and conjuring, of the early and middle ages; compacts with Satan, consorting with evil spirits, and familiarity with the Devil, of later times; all at last ripening into an epidemic demonopathy with its countless victims of fanaticism and error, malevolence and terror, of persecution and ruthless sacrifices.

It is still most potent in its evil, grotesque, and barbaric forms, in Fetichism, Voodooism, Bundooism, Obeahism, and Kahunaism, in the devil and animal ghost worship of the black races, completely exemplified in the arts of the Fetich wizard on the Congo; in the "Uchawi" of the Wasequhha mentioned by Stanley; in the marriage customs of the Soudan devil worshipers; in the practices of the Obeah men and women in the Caribbees—notably their power in matters of love and business, religion and war—in Jamaica; in the incantations of the kahuna in Hawaii; and in the devices of the voodoo or conjure doctor in the southern states; in the fiendish rites and ceremonies of the red men,—the Hoch-e-ayum of the Plains Indians, the medicine dances of the Cheyennes and Arapahoes, the fire dance of the Navajos, the snake dance of the Moquis, the sun dance of the Sioux, in the myths and tales of the Cherokees; and it rings in many tribal chants and songs of the East and West.

It lives as well, and thrives luxuriantly, ripe for the full vintage, in the minds of many people to whom this or that trivial incident or accident of life is an omen of good or evil fortune with a mysterious parentage. Its roots strike deep in that strange element in human nature which dreads whatsoever is weird and uncanny in common experiences, and sees strange portents and dire chimeras in all that is unexplainable to the senses. It is made most virile in the desire for knowledge of the invisible and intangible, that must ever elude the keenest inquiry, a phase of thought always to be reckoned with when imagination runs riot, and potent in its effect, though evanescent as a vision the brain sometimes retains of a dream, and as senseless in the cold light of reason as Monna Sidonia's invocation at the Witches' Sabbath: (*Romance of Leonardo da Vinci,* p. 97, MEREJKOWSKI.)

"Emen Hetan, Emen Hetan, Palu, Baalberi,
Astaroth help us Agora, Agora, Patrisa,
Come and help us."
"Garr-r: Garr-r, up: Don't knock
Your head: We fly: We fly:"

And who may count himself altogether free from the subtle power of the old mystery with its fantastic imageries, when the spirit of unrest is abroad? Who is not moved by it in the awesome stillness of night on the plains, or in the silence of the mountains or of the somber forest aisles; in wild winter nights when old tales are told; in fireside visions as tender memories come and go? And who, when listening to the echoes of the chambers of the restless sea when deep calleth unto deep, does not hear amid them some weird and haunting refrain like Leland's sea song?

"I saw three witches as the wind blew cold
In a red light to the lee;
Bold they were and overbold
As they sailed over the sea;
Calling for One Two Three;
Calling for One Two Three;
And I think I can hear
It a ringing in my ear,
A-calling for the One, Two, Three."

Above all, in its literature does witchcraft exhibit the conclusive proof of its age, its hydra-headed forms, and its influence in the intellectual and spiritual development of the races of men.

What of this literature? Count in it all the works that treat of the subject in its many phases, and its correlatives, and it is limitless, a literature of all times and all lands.

Christian and pagan gave it place in their religions, dogmas, and articles of faith and discipline, and in their codes of law; and for four hundred years, from the appeal of Pope John XXII, in 1320, to extirpate the Devil-worshipers, to the repeal of the statute of James I in 1715, the delusion gave point and force to treatises, sermons, romances, and folk-lore, and invited, nay, compelled, recognition at the hands of the scientist and legist, the historian, the poet and the dramatist, the theologian and philosopher.

But the monographic literature of witchcraft, as it is here considered, is limited, in the opinion of a scholar versed in its lore, to fifteen hundred titles. There is a mass of unpublished materials in libraries and archives at home and abroad, and of information as to witchcraft and the witch trials, accessible in court records, depositions, and current accounts in public and private collections, all awaiting the coming of some master hand to transform them into an exhaustive history of the most grievous of human superstitions.

To this day, there has been no thorough investigation or complete analysis of the history of the witch persecutions. The true story has been distorted by partisanship and ignorance, and left to exploitation by the romancer, the empiric, and the sciolist.

"Of the origin and nature of the delusion we know perhaps enough; but of the causes and paths of its spread, of the extent of its ravages, of its exact bearing upon the intellectual and religious freedom of its times, of the soul-stirring details of the costly struggle by which it was overborne we are lamentably ill informed." (*The Literature of Witchcraft*, p. 66, BURR.)

It must serve in this brief narrative to merely note, within the centuries which marked the climax of the mania, some of the most authoritative and influential works in giving strength to its evil purpose and the modes of accusation, trial, and punishment.

Modern scholarship holds that witchcraft, with the Devil as the arch enemy of mankind for its cornerstone, was first exploited by the Dominicans of the Inquisition. They blazed the tortuous way for the scholastic theology which in the thirteenth and fourteenth centuries gave new recognition to Satan and his satellites as the sworn enemies of God and his church, and the Holy Inquisition with its massive enginery, open and secret, turned its attention to the exposure and extirpation of the heretics and sinners who were enlisted in the Devil's service.

Take for adequate illustration these standard authorities in the early periods of the widespread and virulent epidemic:

Those of the Inquisitor General, Eymeric, in 1359, entitled *Tractatus contra dæmonum*; the Formicarius or Ant Hill of the German Dominican Nider, 1337; the *De calcatione dæmonum*, 1452; the *Flagellum hæreticorum fascinariorum* of the French Inquisitor Jaquier in 1458; and the *Fortalitium fidei* of the Spanish Franciscan Alonso de Spina, in 1459; the famous and infamous manual of arguments and rules of procedure for the detection and punishment of witches, compiled by the German Inquisitors Krämer and Sprenger (Institor) in 1489, buttressed on the bull of Pope Innocent VIII; (this was the celebrated *Witch Hammer*, bearing on its title page the significant legend, "*Not to believe in witchcraft is the greatest of heresies*"); the Canon Episcopi; the bulls of Popes John XXII, 1330, Innocent VIII, 1484, Alexander VI, 1494, Leo X, 1521, and Adrian VI, 1522; the Decretals of the canon law; the exorcisms of the Roman and Greek churches, all hinged on scriptural precedents; the Roman law, the Twelve Tables, and the Justinian Code, the last three imposing upon the crimes of conjuring, exorcising, magical arts, offering sacrifices to the injury of one's neighbors, sorcery, and witchcraft, the penalties of death by torture, fire, or crucifixion.

Add to these classics some of the later authorities: the *Dæmonologie* of the royal inquisitor James I of England and Scotland, 1597; Mores' *Antidote to Atheism*; Fuller's *Holy and Profane State*; Granvil's *Sadducismus Triumphatus*, 1681; *Tryal of Witches at the Assizes for the County of Suffolk before Sir Matthew Hale, March, 1664* (London, 1682); Baxter's *Certainty of the World of Spirits*, 1691; Cotton Mather's *A Discourse on Witchcraft*, 1689, his *Late Memorable Providences Relating to Witchcrafts and Possessions*, 1684, and his *Wonders of the Invisible World*, 1692; and enough references have been made to this literature of delusion, to the precedents that seared the consciences of courts and juries in their sentences of men, women, and children to death by the rack, the wheel, the stake, and the gallows.

Where in history are the horrors of the curse more graphically told than in the words of Canon Linden, an eye witness of the demonic deeds at Trier (Treves) in 1589?

"And so, from court to court throughout the towns and villages of all the diocese, scurried special accusers, inquisitors, notaries, jurors, judges, constables, dragging to trial and torture human beings of both sexes and burning them in great numbers. Scarcely any of those who were accused escaped punishment. Nor were there spared even the leading men in the city of Trier. For the Judge, with two Burgomasters, several Councilors and Associate Judges, canons of sundry collegiate churches, parish-priests, rural deans, were swept away in this ruin. So far, at length, did the madness of the furious populace and of the courts go in this thirst for blood and booty that there was scarcely anybody who was not smirched by some suspicion of this crime.

"Meanwhile notaries, copyists, and innkeepers grew rich. The executioner rode a blooded horse, like a noble of the court, and went clad in gold and silver; his wife vied with noble dames in the richness of her array. The children of those convicted and punished were sent into exile; their goods were confiscated; plowman and vintner failed." (*The Witch Persecutions*, pp. 13-14, BURR.)

Fanaticism did not rule and ruin without hindrance and remonstrance. Men of great learning and exalted position struck mighty blows at the root of the evil. They could not turn the tide but they stemmed it, and their attacks upon the whole theory of Satanic power and the methods of persecution were potent in the reaction to humanity and a reign of reason.

Always to be remembered among these men of power are Johann Wier, Friedrich Spee, and notably Reginald Scot, who in his *Discovery of Witchcraft*, in 1584, undertook to prove that "the contracts and compacts of witches with devils and all infernal spirits and familiars, are but erroneous novelties and erroneous conceptions."

"After all it is setting a high value on our conjectures to roast a man alive on account of them." (MONTAIGNE.)

Who may measure in romance and the drama the presence, the cogent and undeniable power of those same abiding elements of mysticism and mystery, which underlie all human experience, and repeated in myriad forms find their classic expression in the queries of the "Weird Sisters," "*those elemental avengers without sex or kin*"?

"When shall we three meet again,
In thunder, lightning or in rain?
When the hurly burly's done,
When the battle's lost and won."

Are not the mummeries of the witches about the cauldron in Macbeth, and Talbot's threat pour la Pucelle,

"Blood will I draw on thee, thou art a witch,"

uttered so long ago, echoed in the wailing cry of La Meffraye in the forests of Machecoul, in the maledictions of Grio, and of the Saga of the Burning Fields?

Their vitality is also clearly shown in their constant use and exemplification by the romance and novel writers who appeal with certainty and success to the popular taste in the tales of spectral terrors. Witness: Farjeon's *The Turn of the Screw*; Bierce's *The Damned Thing*; Bulwer's *A Strange Story*; Cranford's *Witch of Prague*; Howells' *The Shadow of a Dream*; Winthrop's *Cecil Dreeme*; Grusot's *Night Side of Nature*; Crockett's Black Douglas; and *The Red Axe*, Francis' *Lych-gate Hall*; Caine's *The Shadow of a Crime*; and countless other stories, traditions, tales, and legends, written and unwritten, that invite and receive a gracious hospitality on every hand.

CHAPTER III

"A belief in witchcraft had always existed; it was entertained by Coke, Bacon, Hale and even Blackstone. It was a misdemeanor at English common law and made a felony without benefit of clergy by 33 Henry VIII, c. 8, and 5 Eliz., c. 16, and the more severe statute of I Jas. 1, ch. 12." *Connecticut – Origin of her Courts and Laws* (N.E. States, Vol I, p. 487-488), HAMERSLEY.

"Selden took up a somewhat peculiar and characteristic position. He maintained that the law condemning women to death for witchcraft was perfectly just, but that it was quite unnecessary to ascertain whether witchcraft was a possibility. A woman might not be able to destroy the life of her neighbor by her incantations; but if she intended to do so, it was right that she should be hung." *Rationalism in Europe* (Vol. 1, p. 123) LECKY.

The fundamental authority for legislation, for the decrees of courts and councils as to witchcraft, from the days of the Witch of Endor to those of Mercy Disborough of Fairfield, and Giles Corey of Salem Farms, was the code of the Hebrews and its recognition in the Gospel dispensations. Thereon rest most of the historic precedents, legislative, ecclesiastical, and judicial.

"Thou shalt not suffer a witch to live." Exodus xxii, 18.

What law embalmed in ancientry and honored as of divine origin has been more fruitful of sacrifice and suffering? Through the Scriptures, gathering potency as it goes, runs the same grim decree, with widening definitions.

"And the soul that turneth after such as have familiar spirits and after wizards ... I will even set my face against that soul and will cut him off from among his people." Deuteronomy xviii, 10-11.

"There shall not be found among you any one that maketh his son or his daughter to pass through the fire, or that useth divination, or an observer of times, or an enchanter, or a consulter with familiar spirits, or a wizard, or a necromancer." Deuteronomy xviii, 10-11.

"Saul had put away those that had familiar spirits, and the wizards out of the land." Samuel i, 3.

"Now Saul the king of the Hebrews, had cast out of the country the fortune tellers, and the necromancers, and all such as exercised the like arts, excepting the prophets.... Yet did he bid his servants to inquire out for him some woman that was a necromancer, and called up the souls of the dead, that so he might know whether his affairs would succeed to his mind; for this sort of necromantic women that bring up the souls of the dead, do by them foretell future events." Josephus, Book 6, ch. 14.

"For rebellion is as the sin of witchcraft." Samuel i, 15-23.

"And I will cut off witchcraft out of the land." Micah v. 12.

"Many of them also which used curious arts brought their books together and burned them." Acts xix, 19.

"But there was a certain man called Simon which beforetime in the same city used sorcery and bewitched the people of Samaria." Acts viii, 9.

"If a man abide not in me, he is cast forth as a branch, and is withered, and men gather them and cast them into the fire, and they are burned." [C] John xv, 6.

[C] In the opinion of the eminent Italian jurist Bartolo, witches were burned alive in early times on this authority.

These citations make clear the scriptural recognition of witchcraft as a heinous sin and crime. It is, however, necessary to draw a broad line of demarcation between the ancient forms and manifestations which have been brought into view for an illustrative purpose, and that delusion or mania which centered in the theologic belief and teaching that Satan was the arch enemy of mankind, and clothed with such power over the souls of men as to make compacts with them, and to hold supremacy over them in the warfare between good and evil.

The church from its earliest history looked upon witchcraft as a deadly sin, and disbelief in it as a heresy, and set its machinery in motion for its extirpation. Its authority was the word of God and the civil law, and it claimed jurisdiction through the ecclesiastical courts, the secular courts, however, acting as the executive of their decrees and sentences.

Such was the cardinal principle which governed in the merciless attempts to suppress the epidemic in spreading from the continent to England and Scotland, and at last to the Puritan colonies in America, where the last chapter of its history was written.

There can be no better, no more comprehensive modern definition of the crime once a heresy, or of the popular conception of it, than the one set forth in the New England indictments, to wit: "interteining familiarity with Satan the enemy of mankind, and by his help doing works above the course of nature."

In few words Henry Charles Lea, in his *History of the Inquisition in the Middle Ages*, analyzes the development of the Satanic doctrine from a superstition into its acceptance as a dogma of Christian belief.

"As Satan's principal object in his warfare with God was to seduce human souls from their divine allegiance, he was ever ready with whatever temptation seemed most likely to effect his purpose. Some were to be won by physical indulgence; others by conferring on them powers enabling them apparently to forecast the future, to discover hidden things, to gratify enmity, and to acquire wealth, whether through forbidden arts or by the services of a familiar demon subject to their orders. As the neophyte in receiving baptism renounced the devil, his pomps and his angels, it was necessary for the Christian who desired the aid of Satan to renounce God. Moreover, as Satan when he tempted Christ offered him the kingdoms of the earth in return for adoration—'If thou therefore wilt worship me all shall be thine' (Luke iv, 7)—there naturally arose the idea that to obtain this aid it was necessary to render allegiance to the prince of hell. Thence came the idea, so fruitful in the development of sorcery, of compacts with Satan by which sorcerers became his slaves, binding themselves to do all the evil they could to follow their example. Thus the sorcerer or witch was an enemy of all the human race as well as of God, the most efficient agent of hell in its sempiternal conflict with heaven. His destruction, by any method, was therefore the plainest duty of man.

"This was the perfected theory of sorcery and witchcraft by which the gentle superstitions inherited and adopted from all sides were fitted into the Christian dispensation and formed part of its accepted creed." (*History of Inquisition in the Middle Ages*, 3, 385, LEA.)

Once the widespread superstition became adapted to the forms of religious faith and discipline, and "the prince of the power of the air" was clothed with new energies, the Devil was taken broader account of by Christianity itself; the sorcery of the ancients was embodied in the Christian conception of witchcraft; and the church undertook to deal with it as a heresy; the door was opened wide to the sweep of the epidemic in some of the continental lands.

In Bamburg and Wurzburg, Geneva and Como, Toulouse and Lorraine, and in many other places in Italy, Germany, and France, thousands were sacrificed in the names of religion, justice, and law, with bigotry for their advocate, ignorance for their judge, and fanaticism for their executioner. The storm of demonism raged through three centuries, and was stayed only by the mighty barriers of protest, of inquiry, of remonstrance, and the forces that crystallize and mold public opinion, which guides the destinies of men in their march to a higher civilization.

The flames burning so long and so fiercely on the continent at first spread slowly in England and Scotland. Sorcery in some of its guises had obtained therein ever since the Conquest, and victims had been burned under the king's writ after sentence in the ecclesiastical courts; but witchcraft as a compact with Satan was not made a felony until 1541, by a statute of Henry VIII. Cranmer, in his *Articles of Visitation* in 1549, enjoined the clergy to inquire as to any craft invented by the Devil; and Bishop Jewell, preaching before the queen in 1558, said:

"It may please your Grace to understand that witches and sorcerers within these last few years are marvelously increased within your Grace's realm, Your Grace's subjects pine away even unto the death, their colour fadeth, their flesh rotteth, their speech is benumbed, their senses are bereft."

The act of 1541 was amended in Queen Elizabeth's reign, in 1562, but at the accession of James I—himself a fanatic and bigot in religious matters, and the author of the famous *Dæmonologie*—a new law was enacted with exact definition of the crime, which remained in force more than a hundred years. Its chief provision was this:

"If any person or persons use, practice or exercise any invocation or conjuration of any evil and wicked spirit, or shall consult, covenant with, entertain, employ, feed or reward any evil and wicked spirit to or for any intent or purpose, or take up any dead man, woman, or child out of his, her or their grave, or any other place where the dead body resteth or the skin, bone, or any part of any dead person, to be employed or used in any manner of witchcraft, sorcery, charm, or enchantment, or shall use, practise, or exercise any witchcraft, enchantment, charm, or sorcery, whereby any person shall be killed, destroyed, wasted, consumed, pined or lamed in his or her body or any part thereof: every such offender is a felon without benefit of clergy."

Under this law, and the methods of its administration, witchcraft so called increased; persecutions multiplied, especially under the Commonwealth, and notably in the eastern counties of England, whence so many of all estates, all sorts and conditions of men, had fled over seas to set up the standard of independence in the Puritan colonies.

Many executions occurred in Lancashire, in Suffolk, Essex, and Huntingdonshire, where the infamous scoundrel "Witch-finder-General" Matthew Hopkins, under the sanction of the courts, was "pricking," "waking," "watching," and "testing" persons suspected or accused of witchcraft, with fiendish ingenuity of indignity and torture. Says James Howell in his *Familiar Letters*, in 1646:

"We have multitudes of witches among us; for in Essex and Suffolk there were above two hundred indicted within these two years, and above the half of them executed."

"Within the compass of two years (1645-7), near upon three hundred witches were arraigned, and the major part of them executed in Essex and Suffolk only. Scotland swarms with them more and more, and persons of good quality are executed daily."

Scotland set its seal on witchcraft as a crime by an act of its parliament so early as 1563, amended in 1649. The ministers were the inquisitors and persecutors. They heard the confessions, and inflicted the tortures, and their cruelties were commensurate with the hard and fast theology that froze the blood of mercy in their veins.

The trials were often held by special commissions issued by the privy council, on the petition of a presbytery or general assembly. It was here that those terrible instruments of torture, the caschielawis, the lang irnis, the boot and the pilliewinkis, were used to wring confessions from the wretched victims. It is all a strange and gruesome story of horrors told in detail in the state trial records, and elsewhere, from the execution of Janet Douglas—Lady Glammis—to that of the poor old woman at Dornoch who warmed herself at the fire set for her burning. So firmly seated in the Scotch mind was the belief in witchcraft as a sin and crime, that when the laws against it were repealed in 1736, Scotchmen in the highest stations of church and state remonstrated against the repeal as contrary to the law of God; and William Forbes, in his "Institutes of the Law of Scotland," calls witchcraft "that black art whereby strange and wonderful things are wrought by a power derived from the devil."

This glance at what transpired on the continent and in England and Scotland is of value, in the light it throws on the beliefs and convictions of both Pilgrim and Puritan—Englishmen all—in their new domain, their implicit reliance on established precedents, their credulity in witchcraft matters, and their absolute trust in scriptural and secular authority for their judicial procedure, and the execution of the grim sentences of the courts, until the revolting work of the accuser and the searcher, and the delusion of the ministers and magistrates aflame with mistaken zeal vanished in the sober afterthought, the reaction of the public mind and conscience, which at last crushed the machinations of the Devil and his votaries in high places.

CHAPTER IV

"Hence among all the superstitions that have 'stood over' from primeval ages, the belief in witchcraft has been the most deeply rooted and the most tenacious of life. In all times and places until quite lately, among the most advanced communities, the reality of witchcraft has been accepted without question, and scarcely any human belief is supported by so vast a quantity of recorded testimony."

"Considering the fact that the exodus of Puritans to New England occurred during the reign of Charles I, while the persecutions for witchcraft were increasing toward a maximum in the mother country, it is rather strange that so few cases occurred in the New World." *New France and New England* (pp. 136-144), FISKE.

The forefathers believed in witchcraft—entering into compacts with the Devil—and in all its diabolical subtleties. They had cogent reasons for their belief in example and experience. They set it down in their codes as a capital offense. They found, as has been shown abundant authority in the Bible and in the English precedents. They anchored their criminal codes as they did their theology in the wide and deep haven of the Old Testament decrees and prophecies and maledictions, and doubted not that "the Scriptures do hold forth a perfect rule for the direction and government of all men in all duties which they are to perform to God and men."

Massachusetts, Connecticut, and New Haven, early in their history enacted these capital laws:

In Massachusetts (1641):

"Witchcraft which is fellowship by covenant with a familiar spirit to be punished with death."

"Consulters with witches not to be tolerated, but either to be cut off by death or banishment or other suitable punishment." (*Abstract New England Laws,* 1655.)

In Connecticut (1642):

"If any man or woman be a witch—that is, hath or consulteth with a familiar spirit—they shall be put to death." Exodus xxii, 18; Leviticus xx, 27; Deuteronomy xviii, 10, 11. (*Colonial Records of Connecticut,* Vol. I, p. 77).

In New Haven (1655):

"If any person be a witch, he or she shall be put to death according to" Exodus xxii, 18; Leviticus xx, 27; Deuteronomy xviii, 10, 11. (*New Haven Colonial Records,* Vol. II, p. 576, Cod. 1655).

These laws were authoritative until the epidemic had ceased.

Witches were tried, condemned, and executed with no question as to due legal power, in the minds of juries, counsel, and courts, until the hour of reaction came, hastened by doubts and criticisms of the sources and character of evidence, and the magistrates and clergy halted in their prosecutions and denunciations of an alleged crime born of delusion, and nurtured by a theology run rampant.

"They had not been taught to question the wisdom or the humanity of English criminal law." (*Blue Laws – True and False,* p. 15, TRUMBULL.)

Here and there in New England, following the great immigration from Old England, from 1630-40, during the Commonwealth, and to the Restoration, several cases of witchcraft occurred, but the mania did not set its seal on the minds of men, and inspire them to run amuck in their frenzy, until the days of the swift onset in Massachusetts and Connecticut in 1692, when the zenith of Satan's reign was reached in the Puritan colonies.

A few words about the tragedy at Salem are relevant and essential. They are written because it was the last outbreak of epidemic demonopathy among the civilized peoples; it has been exploited by writers abroad, who have left the dreadful record of the treatment of the delusion in their own countries in the background; it was accompanied in some degree by like manifestations and methods of suppression in sister colonies; it was fanned into flames by men in high station who reveled in its merciless extirpation as a religious duty, and eased their consciences afterwards by contrition, confession and remorse, for their valiant service in the army of the theological devil; and especially for the contrasts it presents to the more cautious and saner methods of procedure that obtained in the governments of Connecticut and New Haven at the apogee of the delusion.

What say the historians and scholars, some of whose ancestors witnessed or participated in the tragedies, and whose acquaintance with the facts defies all challenge?

"It is on the whole the most gruesome episode in American history, and it sheds back a lurid light upon the long tale of witchcraft in the past." (*Fiske's New France and New England*, 195.)

"The sainted minister in the church; the woman of the scarlet letter in the market place! What imagination would have been irreverent enough to surmise that the same scorching stigma was on them both." (*Scarlet Letter*, HAWTHORNE.)

"We are made partners in parish and village feuds. We share in the chimney corner gossip, and learn for the first time how many mean and merely human motives, whether consciously or unconsciously, gave impulse and intensity to the passions of the actors in that memorable tragedy which dealt the death blow in this country to the belief in Satanic compacts." (*Among my Books – Witchcraft*, p. 142, LOWELL.)

"The tragedy was at an end. It lasted about six months, from the first accusations in March until the last executions in September.... It was an epidemic of mad superstitious fear, bitterly to be regretted, and a stain upon the high civilization of the Bay Colony." (*Historic Towns of New England, Salem*, p. 148, LATIMER.)

What was done at Salem, when the tempest of unreason broke loose? Who were the chief actors in it? This was done. From the first accusation in March, 1692, to the last execution in September, 1692, nineteen persons were hanged and one man was pressed to death [D] (*no witch was ever burned in New England*), hundreds of innocent men and women were imprisoned, or fled into exile or hiding places, their homes were broken up, their estates were ruined, and their families and friends were left in sorrow, anxiety, and desolation; and all this terrorism was wrought at the instance of the chief men in the communities, the magistrates, and the ministers.

[D] Fifty-five persons suffered torture, and twenty were executed before the delusion ended. *Ency. Americana* (Vol. 16, "Witchcraft").

Upham in his *Salem Witchcraft* (Vol. II. pp. 249-250) thus pictures the situation.

"The prisons in Salem, Ipswich, Boston, and Cambridge, were crowded. All the securities of society were dissolved. Every man's life was at the mercy of every man. Fear sat on every countenance, terror and distress were in all hearts, silence pervaded the streets; all who could, quit the country; business was at a stand; a conviction sunk into the minds of men, that a dark and infernal confederacy had got foot-hold in the land, threatening to overthrow and extirpate religion and morality, and establish the kingdom of the Prince of darkness in a country which had been dedicated, by the prayers and tears and sufferings of its pious fathers, to the Church of Christ and the service and worship of the true God. The feeling, dismal and horrible indeed, became general, that the providence of God was removed from them; that Satan was let loose, and he and his confederates had free and unrestrained power to go to and fro, torturing and destroying whomever he willed."

The trials were held by a Special Court, consisting of William Stoughton, Peter Sergeant, Nath. Saltonstall, Wait Winthrop, Bartho' Gedney, John Richards, Saml. Sewall, John Hathorne, Tho. Newton, and Jonathan Corwin,—not one of them a lawyer.

Whatever his associates may have thought of their ways of doing God's service, after the tragedy was over, Sewall, one of the most zealous of the justices, made a public confession of his errors before the congregation of the Old South Church, January 14, 1697. Were the agonizing groans of poor old Giles Corey, pressed to death under planks weighted with stones, or the prayers of the saintly Burroughs ringing in his ears?

"The conduct of Judge Sewall claims our particular admiration. He observed annually in private a day of humiliation and prayer, during the remainder of his life, to keep fresh in his mind a sense of repentance and sorrow for the part he bore in the trials. On the day of the general fast, he arose in the place where he was accustomed to worship, the old South, in Boston, and in the presence of the great assembly, handed up to the pulpit a written confession, acknowledging the error into which he had been led, praying for the forgiveness of God and his people, and concluding with a request, to all the congregation to unite with him in devout supplication, that it might not bring down the displeasure of the Most High upon his country, his family, or himself. He remained standing during the public reading of the paper. This was an act of true manliness and dignity of soul." (*Upham's Salem Witchcraft*, Vol. II, p. 441).

Grim, stern, narrow as he was, this man in his self-judgment commands the respect of all true men.

The ministers stood with the magistrates in their delusion and intemperate zeal. Two hundred and sixteen years after the last witch was hung in Massachusetts a clearer light falls on one of the striking personalities of the time—Cotton Mather—who to a recent date has been credited with the chief responsibility for the Salem prosecutions.

Did he deserve it?

Robert Calef, in his *More Wonders of the Invisible World*, Bancroft in his *History of the United States*, and Charles W. Upham in his *Salem Witchcraft*, are the chief writers who have placed Mather in the foreground of those dreadful scenes, as the leading minister of the time, an active personal participant in the trials and executions, and a zealot in the maintenance of the ministerial dignity and domination.

On the other hand, the learned scholar, the late William Frederick Poole, first in the *North American Review*, in 1869, and again in his paper *Witchcraft in Boston*, in 1882, in the *Memorial History of Boston*, calls Calef an immature youth, and says that his obvious intent, and that of the several unknown contributors who aided him, was to malign the Boston ministers and to make a sensation.

And the late John Fiske, in his *New France and New England* (p. 155), holds that:

"Mather's rules (of evidence) would not have allowed a verdict of guilty simply upon the drivelling testimony of the afflicted persons, and if this wholesome caution had been observed, not a witch would ever have been hung in Salem."

What were those rules of evidence and of procedure attributed to Mather? Through the Special Court appointed to hold the witch trials, and early in its sittings, the opinions of twelve ministers of Boston and vicinity were asked as to witchcraft. Cotton Mather wrote and his associates signed an answer June 15, 1692, entitled, *The Return of Several Ministers Consulted by his Excellency and the Honorable Council upon the Present Witchcrafts in Salem Village*. This was the opinion of the ministers, and it is most important to note what is said in it of spectral evidence, [E] as it was upon such evidence that many convictions were had:

"1. The afflicted state of our poor neighbors that are now suffering by molestations from the Invisible World we apprehend so deplorable, that we think their condition calls for the utmost help of all persons in their several capacities.

"2. We cannot but with all thankfulness acknowledge the success which the merciful God has given unto the sedulous and assiduous endeavors of our honorable rulers to detect the abominable witchcrafts which have been committed in the country; humbly praying that the discovery of these mysterious and mischievous wickednesses may be perfected.

"3. We judge that, in the prosecution of these and all such witchcrafts there is need of a very critical and exquisite caution, lest by too much credulity for things received only upon the devil's authority, there be a door opened for a long train of miserable consequences, and Satan get an advantage over us; for we should not be ignorant of his devices.

"4. As in complaints upon witchcraft there may be matters of inquiry which do not amount unto matters of presumption, and there may be matters of presumption which yet may not be matters of conviction, so it is necessary that all proceedings thereabout be managed with an exceeding tenderness toward those that may be complained of, especially if they have been persons formerly of an unblemished reputation.

"5. When the first inquiry is made into the circumstances of such as may lie under the just suspicion of witchcrafts, we could wish that there may be admitted as little as possible of such noise, company and openness as may too hastily expose them that are examined, and that there may be nothing used as a test for the trial of the suspected, the lawfulness whereof may be doubted by the people of God, but that the directions given by such judicious writers as Perkins and Barnard may be observed.

"6. Presumptions whereupon persons may be committed, and much more, convictions whereupon persons may be condemned as guilty of witchcrafts, ought certainly to be more considerable than barely the accused persons being represented by a spectre unto the afflicted, inasmuch as it is an undoubted and notorious thing that a demon may by God's permission appear even to ill purposes, in the shape of an innocent, yea, and a virtuous man. Nor can we esteem alterations made in the sufferers, by a look or touch of the accused, to be an infallible evidence of guilt, but frequently liable to be abused by the devil's legerdemains.

"7. We know not whether some remarkable affronts given the devils, by our disbelieving these testimonies whose whole force and strength is from them alone, may not put a period unto the progress of the dreadful calamity begun upon us, in the accusation of so many persons whereof some, we hope, are yet clear from the great transgression laid to their charge.

"8. Nevertheless, we cannot but humbly recommend unto the government, the speedy and vigorous prosecutions of such as have rendered themselves obnoxious, according to the directions given in the laws of God and the wholesome statutes of the English nation for the detection of witchcrafts."

[E] An illustration: The child Ann Putnam, in her testimony against the Rev. Mr. Burroughs, said that one evening the apparition of a minister came to her and asked her to write her name in the devil's book. Then came the forms of two women in winding sheets, and looked angrily upon the minister and scolded him until he was fain to vanish away. Then the women told Ann that they were the ghosts of Mr. Burroughs' first and second wives whom he had murdered.

Did Longfellow, after a critical study of the original evidence and records, truly interpret Mather's views, in his dialogue with Hathorne?

MATHER:
"Remember this, That as a sparrow falls not to the ground
Without the will of God, so not a Devil
Can come down from the air without his leave.
We must inquire."
HATHORNE:
"Dear sir, we have inquired;
Sifted the matter thoroughly through and through,
And then resifted it."
MATHER:
"If God permits
These evil spirits from the unseen regions
To visit us with surprising informations,
We must inquire what cause there is for this,
But not receive the testimony borne
By spectres as conclusive proof of guilt
In the accused."
HATHORNE:

"Upon such evidence
We do not rest our case. The ways are many
In which the guilty do betray themselves."
MATHER:
"Be careful, carry the knife with such exactness
That on one side no innocent blood be shed
By too excessive zeal, and on the other
No shelter given to any work of darkness."
New England Tragedies (4, 725), LONGFELLOW.

Whatever Mather's caution to the court may have been, or his leadership in learning, or his ambition and his clerical zeal, there is thus far no evidence, in all his personal participation in the tragedies, that he lifted his hand to stay the storm of terrorism once begun, or cried halt to the magistrates in their relentless work. On the contrary, after six victims had been executed, August 4, 1692, in *A Discourse on the Wonders of the Invisible World*, Mather wrote this in deliberate, cool afterthought:

"They—the judges—have used as judges have heretofore done, the spectral evidences, to introduce their farther inquiries into the lives of the persons accused; and they have thereupon, by the wonderful Providence of God, been so strengthened with other evidences that some of the witch-gang have been fairly executed."

And a year later, in the light of all his personal experience and investigation, Mather solemnly declared:

"If in the midst of the many dissatisfactions among us, the publication of these trials may promote such a pious thankfulness unto God for justice being so far executed among us, I shall rejoice that God is glorified."

Wherever the responsibility at Salem may have rested, the truth is that in the general fear and panic there was potent in the minds, both of the clergy and the laity, the spirit of fanaticism and malevolence in some instances, such as misled the pastor of the First Church to point to the corpses of Giles Corey's devoted and saintly wife and others swinging to and fro, and say "What a sad thing it is to see eight firebrands of hell hanging there."

This conspectus of witchcraft, old and new, of its development from the sorcery and magic of the ancients into the mediæval theological dogma of the power of Satan, of its gradual ripening into an epidemic demonopathy, of its slow growth in the American colonies, of its volcanic outburst in the close of the seventeenth century, is relevant and appropriate to this account of the delusion in Connecticut, its rise and suppression, its firm hold on the minds and consciences of the colonial leaders for threescore years after the settlement of the towns, a chapter in Connecticut history written in the presence of the actual facts now made known and available, and with a purpose of historic accuracy.

CHAPTER V

"It was not to be expected of the colonists of New England that they should be the first to see through a delusion which befooled the whole civilized world, and the gravest and most knowing persons in it. The colonists in Connecticut and New Haven, as well as in Massachusetts, like all other Christian people at that time—at least with extremely rare individual exceptions—believed in the reality of a hideous crime called witchcraft." PALFREY'S *New England* (Vol. IV, pp. 96-127).

"The truth is that it [witchcraft] pervaded the whole Christian Church. The law makers and the ministers of New England were under its influences as—and no more than—were the law makers and ministers of Old England." *Blue Laws – True and False* (p. 23), TRUMBULL.

"One ---- of Windsor Arraigned and Executed at Hartford for a Witch." WINTHROP'S *Journal* (2: 374, Savage Ed., 1853).

Here beginneth the first chapter of the story of the delusion in Connecticut. It is an entry made by John Winthrop, Governor of the Massachusetts Bay Colony, in his famous journal, without specific date, but probably in the spring of 1647.

It is of little consequence save as much has been made of it by some writers as fixing the relative date of the earliest execution for witchcraft in New England, and locating it in one of the three original Connecticut towns.

What matters it at this day whether Mary Johnson as tradition runs, or Alse Youngs as truth has it, was put to death for witchcraft in Windsor, Connecticut, in 1647, or Martha Jones of Charlestown, Massachusetts, was hung for the same crime at Boston in 1648, as also set down in Winthrop's Journal?

"It may possibly be thought a great neglect, or matter of partiality, that no account is given of witchcraft in Connecticut. The only reason is, that after the most careful researches, no indictment of any person for that crime, nor any process relative to that affair can be found." (*History of Connecticut,* 1799, Preface, BENJAMIN TRUMBULL, D.D.)

"A few words should be said regarding the author's mention of the subject of witchcraft in Connecticut.... It is, I believe, strictly true, as he says 'that no indictment of any person for that crime nor any process relative to that affair can be found.'

"It must be confessed, however, that a careful study of the official colonial records of Connecticut and New Haven leaves no doubt that Goodwife Bassett was convicted and hung at Stratford for witchcraft in 1651, and Goodwife Knapp at Fairfield in 1653. It is also recorded in Winthrop's *Journal* that 'One ---- of Windsor was arraigned and executed at Hartford for a witch' in March, 1646-47, which if it actually occurred, forms the first instance of an execution for witchcraft in New England. The quotation here given is the only known authority for the statement, and opens the question whether something probably recorded as hearsay in a journal, may be taken as authoritative evidence of an occurrence.... The fact however remains, that the official records are as our author says, silent regarding the actual proceedings, and it is only by inference that it may be found from these records that the executions took place." (Introduction to Reprint of *Trumbull's History of Connecticut,* 1898, JONATHAN TRUMBULL.)

The searcher for inerrant information about witchcraft in Connecticut may easily be led into a maze of contradictions, and the statement last above quoted is an apt illustration, with record evidence to the contrary on every hand. Tradition, hearsay, rumor, misstatements, errors, all colored by ignorance or half knowledge, or a local jealousy or pride, have been woven into a woof of precedent and acceptance, and called history.

As has been already stated, the general writers from Trumbull to Johnston have nothing of value to say on the subject; the open official records and the latest history—*Connecticut as a Colony and a State*—cover only certain cases, and nowhere from the beginning to this day has the story of witchcraft been fully told.

Connecticut can lose nothing in name or fame or honor, if, more than two centuries after the last witch was executed within her borders, the facts as to her share in the strange superstition be certified from the current records of the events.

How may this story best be told? Clearly, so far as may be, in the very words of the actors in those tragic scenes, in the words of the minister and magistrate, the justice and the juryman, the accuser and the accused, and the searcher. Into this court of inquiry come all these personalities to witness the sorrowful march of the victims to the scaffold or to exile, or to acquittal and deliverance with the after life of suspicion and social ostracism.

The spectres of terror did not sit alone at the firesides of the poor and lowly: they stalked in high places, and were known of men and women of the first rank in education and the social virtues, and of greatest influence in church and state.

Of this fact there is complete demonstration in a glance at the dignitaries who presided at one of the earliest witchcraft trials—men of notable ancestry, of learning, of achievements, leaders in colonial affairs, whose memories are honored to this day.

These were the magistrates at a session entitled "A particular courte in Hartford upon the tryall of John Carrington and his wife 20th Feb., 1662" (See *Rec. P.C.*, 2: 17): Edw. Hopkins Esqr., Gournor John Haynes Esqr. Deputy, Mr. Wells, Mr. Woolcott, Mr. Webster, Mr. Cullick, Mr. Clarke.

This court had jurisdiction over misdemeanors, and was "aided by a jury," as a close student of colonial history, the late Sherman W.

Adams, quaintly says in one of his historical papers. These were the jurymen:

Mr. Phelps	John White	John More
Mr. Tailecoat	Will Leawis	Edw. Griswold
Mr. Hollister	Sam. Smith	Steph. Harte
Daniel Milton	John Pratt	Theo. Judd

Before this tribunal—representative of the others doing like service later—made up of the foremost citizens, and of men in the ordinary walks of life, endowed with hard common sense and presumably inspired with a spirit of justice and fair play, came John Carrington and his wife Joan of Wethersfield, against whom the jury brought in a verdict of guilty.

It must be clearly borne in mind that all these men, in this as in all the other witchcraft trials in Connecticut, illustrious or commonplace—as are many of their descendants whose names are written on the rolls of the patriotic societies in these days of ancestral discovery and exploitation—were absolute believers in the powers of Satan and his machinations through witchcraft and the evidence then adduced to prove them, and trained to such credulity by their education and experience, by their theological doctrines, and by the law of the land in Old England, but still clothed upon with that righteousness which as it proved in the end made them skeptical as to certain alleged evidences of guilt, and swift to respond to the calls of reason and of mercy when the appeals were made to their calm judgment and second thought as to the sins of their fellowmen.

In no way can the truth be so clearly set forth, the real character of the evidence be so justly appreciated upon which the convictions were had, as from the depositions and the oral testimony of the witnesses themselves. They are lasting memorials to the credulity and superstition, and the religious insanity which clouded the senses of the wisest men for a time, and to the malevolence and satanic ingenuity of the people who, possessed of the devil accused their friends and neighbors of a crime punishable by death.

Nor is this dark chapter in colonial history without its flashes of humor and ridiculousness, as one follows the absurd and unbridled testimonies which have been chosen as completely illustrative of the whole series in the years of the witchcraft nightmare. They are in part cited here, for the sake of authenticity and exactness, as written out in the various court records and depositions, published and unpublished, in the ancient style of spelling, and are worthy the closest study for many reasons.

It will, however, clear the way to a better understanding of the unique testimonies of the witch witnesses, if there be first presented the authoritative reasons for the examination of a witch, coupled with a summary of the lawful tests of innocence or guilt. They are in the handwriting of William Jones, a Deputy Governor of Connecticut and a member of the court at some of the trials.

GROUNDS FOR EXAMINATION OF A WITCH

"1. Notorious defamacon by ye common report of the people a ground of suspicion.

"2. Second ground for strict examinacon is if a fellow witch gave testimony on his examinacon or death yt such a pson is a witch, but this is not sufficient for conviccon or condemnacon.

"3. If after cursing, there follow death or at least mischiefe to ye party.

"4. If after quarrelling or threatening a prsent mischiefe doth follow for ptye's devilishly disposed after cursing doe use threatnings, & yt alsoe is a grt prsumcon agt y.

"5. If ye pty suspected be ye son or daughter, the serv't or familiar friend, neer neighbors or old companion of a knowne or convicted witch this alsoe is a prsumcon, for witchcraft is an art yt may be larned & covayd from man to man & oft it falleth out yt a witch dying leaveth som of ye aforesd heires of her witchcraft.

"6. If ye pty suspected have ye devills mark for t'is thought wn ye devill maketh his covent with y he alwayess leaves his mark behind him to know y for his owne yt is, if noe evident reason in can be given for such mark.

"7. Lastly if ye pty examined be unconstant & contrary to himselfe in his answers.

"Thus much for examinacon wch usually is by Q. & some tymes by torture upon strong & grt presumcon.

"For conviccon it must be grounded on just and sufficient proofes. The proofes for conviccon of 2 sorts, 1, Some be less sufficient, some more sufficient.

"Less sufficient used in formr ages by red hot iron and scalding water. ye pty to put in his hand in one or take up ye othr, if not hurt ye pty cleered, if hurt convicted for a witch, but this was utterly condemned. In som countryes anothr proofe justified by some of ye learned by casting ye pty bound into water, if she sanck counted inocent, if she sunk not yn guilty, but all those tryalls the author counts supstitious and unwarrantable and worse. Although casting into ye water is by some justified for ye witch having made a ct wth ye devill she hath renounced her baptm & hence ye antipathy between her & water, but this he makes nothing off. Anothr insufficient testimoy of a witch is ye testimony of a wizard, who prtends to show ye face of ye witch to ye party afflicted in a glass, but this he counts diabolicall & dangerous, ye devill may reprsent a pson inocent. Nay if after curses & threats mischiefe follow or if a sick pson like to dy take it on his death such a one has bewitched him, there are strong grounds of suspicon for strict examinacon but not sufficient for conviccon.

"But ye truer proofes sufficient for conviccon are ye voluntary confession of ye pty suspected adjudged sufficient proofe by both divines & lawyers. Or 2 the testimony of 2 witnesses of good and honest report avouching things in theire knowledge before ye magistrat 1 wither yt ye party accused hath made a league wth ye devill or 2d or hath ben some knowne practices of witchcraft. Argumts to prove either must be as 1 if they can pve ye pty hath invocated ye devill for his help this pt of yt ye devill binds withes to.

"Or 2 if ye pty hath entertained a familiar spt in any forme mouse cat or othr visible creature.

"Or 3 if they affirm upon oath ye pty hath done any accon or work wch inferreth a ct wth ye devill, as to shew ye face of a man in a glass, or used inchantmts or such feates, divineing of things to come, raising tempests, or causing ye forme of a dead man to appeare or ye like it sufficiently pves a witch.

"But altho those are difficult things to prove yet yr are wayes to come to ye knowledg of y, for tis usuall wth Satan to pmise anything till ye league be ratified, & then he nothing ye discovery of y, for wtever witches intend the devill intends nothing but theire utter confusion, therefore in ye just judgmt of God it soe oft falls out yt some witches shall by confession discour ys, or by true testimonies be convicted.

"And ye reasons why ye devill would discover y is 1 his malice towards all men 2 his insatiable desire to have ye witches not sure enough of y till yn.

"And ye authors warne jurors, &c not to condemne suspected psons on bare prsumtions wthout good & sufficient proofes.

"But if convicted of yt horrid crime to be put to death, for God hath said thou shalt not suffer a witch to live."

The accuser and the prosecutor were aided in their work in a peculiar way. It was the theory and belief that every witch was marked—very privately marked—by the Devil, and the marks could only be discovered by a personal examination. And thus there came into the service of the courts a servant known as a "searcher," usually a woman, as most of the unfortunates who were accused were women.

The location and identification of the witch marks involved revolting details, some of the reports being unprintable. It is, however, indispensable to a right understanding of the delusion and the popular opinions which made it possible, that these incidents, abhorrent and nauseating as they are, be given within proper limitations to meet inquiry—not curiosity—and because they may be noted in various records.

A standard authority in legal procedure in England, recognized in witchcraft prosecutions in the New England colonies, was *Dal-*

ton's Country Justice, first published in 1619 in England, and in its last edition in 1746.

In its chapter on Witchcraft are these directions as to the witch marks:

"These witches have ordinarily a familiar, or spirit which appeareth to them, sometimes in one shape and sometimes in another; as in the shape of a man, woman, boy, dog, cat, foal, hare, rat, toad, etc. And to these their spirits, they give names, and they meet together to christen them (as they speak).... And besides their sucking the Devil leaveth other marks upon their body, sometimes like a blue or red spot, like a flea-biting, sometimes the flesh sunk in and hollow. And these Devil's marks be insensible, and being pricked will not bleed, and be often in their secretest parts, and therefore require diligent and careful search. These first two are main points to discover and convict those witches."

These methods were adopted in the proceedings against witches in Connecticut, and it will suffice to cite one of the reports of a committee—Sarah Burr, Abigail Burr, Abigail Howard, Sarah Wakeman, and Hannah Wilson,—"apointed (by the court) to make sarch upon ye bodis of Marcy Disbrough and Goodwif Clauson," at Fairfield, in September and October 1692, sworn to before Jonathan Bell, Commissioner, and John Allyn, Secretary.

"Wee Sarah bur and abigall bur and Abigail howard and Sarah wakman all of fayrfeild with hanna wilson being by order of authority apointed to make sarch upon ye bodis of marcy disbrough and goodwif Clauson to see what they Could find on ye bodies of ether & both of them; and wee retor as followeth and doe testify as to goodwif Clauson forementioned wee found on her secret parts Just within ye lips of ye same growing within sid sumewhat as broad and reach without ye lips of ye same about on Inch and half long lik in shape to a dogs eare which wee apprehend to be vnvsuall to women.

"and as to marcy wee find on marcy foresayd on her secret parts growing within ye lep of ye same a los pees of skin and when puld it is near an Inch long somewhat in form of ye fingar of a glove flatted "that lose skin wee Judge more than common to women."

"Octob. 29 1692 The above sworn by the above-named as attests

"JOHN ALLYN Secry"

CHAPTER VI

"Remembering all this, it is not surprising that witches were tried, convicted and put to death in New England; and the manner in which the waning superstition was dealt with by Connecticut lawyers and ministers is the more significant of that robust common sense, rejection of superstition, political and religious, and fearless acceptance of the ethical mandates of the great Lawgiver, which influenced the growth of their jurisprudence and stamped it with an unmistakable individuality." *Connecticut; Origin of her Courts and Laws* (N.E. States, 1: 487-488), HAMERSLEY.

"They made witch-hunting a branch of their social police, and desire for social solidarity. That this was wrong and mischievous is granted; but it is ordinary human conduct now as then. It was a most illogical, capricious, and dangerous form of enforcing punishment, abating nuisances, and shutting out disagreeable truths; fertile in injustice, oppression, the shedding of innocent blood, and the extinguishing of light. No one can justify it, or plead beneficial results from it which could not have been secured with far less evil in other ways. But it was natural that, believing the crime to exist, they should use the belief to strike down offenders or annoyances out of reach of any other *legal* means. They did not invent the crime for the purpose, nor did they invent the death penalty for this crime." *Connecticut as a Colony* (1: 206), MORGAN.

"As to what you mention, concerning that poor creature in your town that is afflicted and mentioned my name to yourself and son, I return you hearty thanks for your intimation about it, and for your charity therein mentioned; and I have great cause to bless God, who, of his mercy hitherto, hath not left me to fall into such an horrid evil." Extract of a Letter from Sec. Allyn to Increase Mather, Hartford, Mar. 18, 1692-93.

An accusation of witchcraft was a serious matter, one of life or death, and often it was safer to become an accuser than one of the accused. Made in terror, malice, mischief, revenge, or religious dementia, or of some other ingredients in the Devil's brew, it passed through the stages of suspicion, espionage, watchings, and searchings, to the formal complaints and indictments which followed the testimony of the witnesses, in their madness and delusion hotfoot to tell the story of their undoing, their grotesque imaginings, their spectral visions, their sufferings at the hands of Satan and his tools, and all aimed at people, their neighbors and acquaintances, often wholly innocent, but having marked personal peculiarities, or of irregular lives by the Puritan standard, or unpopular in their communities, who were made the victim of one base passion or another and brought to trial for a capital offense against person and property.

Taking into account the actual number of accusations, trials, and convictions or acquittals, the number of witnesses called and depositions given was very great. And the later generations owe their opportunity to judge aright in the matter, to the foresight of the men of chief note in the communities who saw the vital necessity of record evidence, and so early as 1666, in the General Court of Connecticut, it was ordered that

"Whatever testimonies are improved in any court of justice in this corporation in any action or case to be tried, shall be presented in writing, and so kept by the secretary or clerk of the said court on file."

This preliminary analysis brings the searcher for the truth face to face with the very witnesses who have left behind them, in the attested records, the ludicrous or solemn, the pitiable or laughable memorials of their own folly, delusion, or deviltry, which marked them then and now as Satan's chosen servitors.

Among the many witnesses and their statements on oath now made available, the chief difficulty is one of selection and elimination; and there will be presented here with the context some of the chief depositions [F] and statements in the most notable witchcraft trials in some of the Connecticut towns, that are typical of all of them, and show upon what travesties of evidence the juries found their verdicts and the courts imposed their sentences.

[F] The selected testimonies herein given are from the Connecticut and New Haven colonial records; from the original depositions in some of the witchcraft cases, in manuscript, a part of the *Wyllys Papers*, so called, now in the Connecticut State Library; and from the notes and papers on witchcraft of the late Charles J. Hoadley, LL.D., compiler of the colonial and state records, and for nearly a half century the state librarian.

KATHERINE (KATERAN) HARRISON

At a Court of Assistants held at Hartford May 11, 1669, presided over by Maj. John Mason—the conqueror of the Pequots—then Deputy Governor, Katherine Harrison, after an examination by the court on a charge of suspicion of witchcraft, was committed to the common jail, to be kept in durance until she came to trial and deliverance by the law.

At an adjourned session of the court at Hartford, May 25, 1669, presided over by John Winthrop, Governor, with William Leete, Deputy Governor, Major Mason and others as assistants, an indictment was found against the prisoner in these words:

"Kateran Harrison thou standest here indicted by ye name of Kateran Harrison (of Wethersfield) as being guilty of witchcraft for that thou not haueing the fear of God before thine eyes hast had familiaritie with Sathan the grand enemie of god and mankind and by his help hast acted things beyond and beside the ordinary course of nature and hast thereby hurt the bodyes of divers of the subjects of or souraigne Lord the King of which by the law of god and of this corporation thou oughtest to dye."

Katherine plead not guilty and "refered herself to a tryall by the jury present," to whom this solemn oath was administered:

"You doe sware by the great and dreadful name of the everliuing god that you will well and truely try just verdict give and true deliverance make between or Souraigne Lord the King and such prisoner or prisoners at the barr as shall be given you in charge according to the Evidence given in Court and the lawes so help you god in or lord Jesus."

A partial trial was had at the May session of the court, but the jury could not agree upon a verdict, and adjournment was had until the October session, when a verdict was to be given in, and the prisoner was remanded to remain in prison in the meantime.

It seems incredible that men like Winthrop and Mason, Treat and Leete, and others of the foremost rank in those days, could have served as judges in such trials, and in all earnestness and sincerity listened to and given credence to the drivel, the travesties of common sense, the mockeries of truth, which fell from the lips of the witnesses in their testimonies. Some of the absurd charges against Katherine Harrison invite particular attention and need no comment. They speak for themselves.

THOMAS BRACY (probably Tracy)—*Misfit jacket and breeches—Vision of the red calf's head—Murderous counsel—"Afflictinge"*

"Thomas Bracy aged about 31 years testifieth as follows that formerly James Wakeley would haue borrowed a saddle of the saide Thomas Bracy, which Thomas Bracy denyed to lend to him, he threatened Thomas and saide, it had bene better he had lent it to him. Allsoe Thomas Bracy beinge at worke the same day making a jacket & a paire of breeches, he labored to his best understanding to set on the sleeues aright on the jacket and seauen tymes he placed the sleues wronge, setting the elbow on the wronge side and was faine to rip them of and new set them on againe, and allsoe the breeches goeing to cut out the breeches, haueing two peices of cloth of different collors, he was soe bemoydered in the matter, that he cut the breeches one of one collor the other off another collor, in such a manner he was bemoydered in his understandinge or actinge yet neuertheless the same daie and tyme he was well in his understandinge and health in other matters and soe was forced to leaue workinge that daie.

"The said Thomas beinge at Sargant Hugh Wells his house ouer against John Harrison's house, in Weathersfield, he saw a cart cominge towards John Harrisons house loaden wth hay, on the top of the hay he saw perfectly a red calfes head, the eares standing peart up, and keeping his sight on the cart tell the cart came to the barne, the calfe vanised, and Harrison stoode on the carte wch appared not to Thomas before, nor could Thomas find or see any calfe theire at all though he sought to see the calfe.

"After this Thomas Bracy giuing out some words, that he suspected Katherin Gooddy Harrison of witchcraft, Katherin Harrison mett Thomas Bracy and threatned Thomas telling him that shee would be euen with him. After that Thomas Bracy aforesaide, being well in his sences & health and perfectly awake, his brothers in bed with him, Thomas aforesaid saw the saide James Wakely and the saide Katherin Harrison stand by his bed side, consultinge to kill him the said Thomas, James Wakely said he would cut his throate, but Katherin counselled to strangle him, presently the said Katherin seised on Thomas striuinge to strangle him, and pulled or pinched him so as if his flesh had been pulled from his bones, theirefore Thomas groaned. At length his father Marten heard and spake, then Thomas left groninge and lay quiet a little, and then Katherin fell againe to afflictinge and pinching, Thomas againe groninge Mr. Marten heard and arose and came to Thomas whoe could not speake till Mr. Marten laid his hands on Thomas, then James and Katherin aforesaid went to the beds feete, his father Marten and his mother stayed watchinge by Thomas all that night after, and the next day Mr. Marten and his wife saw the mark of the saide afflictinge and pinchinge."

"Dated 13th of August one thousand six hundred sixtie and eight.

"Hadley. Taken upon oath before us.

"HENRY CLARKE. "SAMUELL SMITH."

JOSEPH DICKINSON—*Voice calling Hoccanum! Hoccanum! Hoccanum!--A far cry—Cows running "taile on end"*

"The deposition of Joseph Dickenson of Northampton, aged about 32 years, testifieth that he and Philip Smith of Hadley went down early in the morninge to the greate dry swampe, and theire we heard a voice call Hoccanum, Hoccanum, Come Hoccanum, and coming further into the swampe wee see that it was Katherin Harrison that caled as before. We saw Katherin goe from thence homewards. The said Philip parted from Joseph, and a small tyme after Joseph met Philip againe, and then the said Philip affirmed that he had seene Katherin's cows neare a mile from the place where Katherin called them. The saide Joseph went homewards, and goeing homeward met Samuell Bellden ridinge into or downe the meadow. Samuel Belden asked Joseph wheather he had seene the saide Katherin Harrison & the saide Samuel told Joseph aforesaide that he saw her neare the meadow gate, going homeward, and allso more told him that he saw Katherin Harrison her cows runninge with greate violence, taile on end, homewards, and said he thought the cattell would be at home soe soon as Katherin aforesaid if they could get out at the meadow gate, and further this deponent saieth not" Northampton, 13, 6, 1668, taken upon oth before us, William Clarke David Wilton. Exhibited in court Oct. 29, 1668. Attests John Allyn, Secry.

RICHARD MOUNTAGUE—*Over the great river to Nabuck—The mystery of the swarming bees*

"Richard Mountague, aged 52 years, testifieth as followeth, that meeting with Goodwife Harrison in Weathersfield the saide Katherin Harrison saide that a swarm of her beese flew away over her neighbour Boreman's lott and into the great meadow, and thence over the greate river to Nabuck side, but the said Katherin saide that shee had fetched them againe; this seemed very strange to the saide Richard, because this was acted in a little tyme and he did believe the said Katherin neither went nor used any lawful meanes to fetch the said beese as aforesaid." Dated the 13 of August, 1668. Hadley, taken upon oath before us, Henry Clarke, Samuel Smith. Exhibited in Court, October 29: 68, as attests John Allyn Secretry.

JOHN GRAVES—*Bucolic reflections – The trespass on his neighbor's "rowing" – The cartrope adventure – The runaway oxen*

"John Graves aged about 39 years testifieth that formerly going to reap in the meadow at Wethersfield, his land he was to work on lay near to John Harrison's land. It came into the thoughts of the said John Graves that the said John Harrison and Katherine his wife being rumored to be suspicious of witchcraft, therefore he would graze his cattle on the rowing of the land of goodman Harrison, thinking that if the said Harrisons were witches then something would disturb the quiet feeding of the cattle. He thereupon adventured and tied his oxen to his cart rope, one to one end and the other to the other end, making the oxen surely fast as he could, tieing 3 or 4 fast knots at each end, and tying his yoke to the cartrope about the middle of the rope between the oxen; and himself went about 10 or 12 pole distant, to see if the cattle would quietly feed as in other places. The cattle stood staring and fed not, and looking stedfastly on them he saw the cartrope of its own accord untie and fall to the ground; thereupon he went and tied the rope more fast and more knots in it and stood apart as before to see the issue. In a little time the oxen as affrighted fell to running, and ran with such violence that he judgeth that the force and speed of their running made the yoke so tied fly above six foot high to his best discerning. The cattle were used ordinarily before to be so tied and fed—in other places, & presently after being so tied on other men's ground they fed—peaceably as at other times." Dated August, 1668. Hadley; taken upon oath before us Henry Clarke, Samuel Smith. Exhibited in court Oct. 29th, 1668, attests John Allyn, Sec.

JOANE FRANCIS—*The sick child – The spectre*

Joane Francis her testimony. "About 4 years ago, about the beginning of November, in the night just before my child was struck ill, goodwife Harrison or her shape appeared, and I said, the Lord bless me and my child, here is goody Harrison. And the child lying on the outside I took it and laid it between me and my husband. The child continued strangely ill about three weeks, wanting a day, and then died, had fits. We felt a thing run along the sides or side like a whetstone. Robert Francis saith he remembers his wife said that night the child was taken ill, the Lord bless me and my child, here is goody Harrison."

JACOB JOHNSON'S WIFE—*The box on the head—Diet, drink, and plasters—Epistaxis*

"The relation of the wife of Jacob Johnson. She saith that her former husband was employed by goodman Harrison to go to Windsor with a canoe for meal, and he told me as he lay in his bed at Windsor in the night he had a great box on the head, and after when he came home he was ill, and goodwife Harrison did help him with diet drink and plasters, but after a while we sent to Capt. Atwood to help my husband in his distress, but the same day that he came at night I came in at the door, & to the best of my apprehension I saw the likeness of goodwife Harrison with her face towards my husband, and I turned about to lock the door & she vanist away. Then my husband's nose fell a bleeding in an extraordinary manner, & so continued (if it were meddled with) to his dying day. Sworn in court Oct. 29, 1668, attests John Allyn, Secy."

MARY HALE—Noises and blows—The canine apparition—The voice in the night—The Devil a liar

"That about the latter end of November, being the 29th day, 1668, the said Mary Hale lying in her bed, a good fire giving such light that one might see all over that room where the said Mary then was, the said Mary heard a noise, & presently something fell on her legs with such violence that she feared it would have broken her legs, and then it came upon her stomach and oppressed her so as if it would have pressed the breath out of her body. Then appeared an ugly shaped thing like a dog, having a head such that I clearly and distinctly knew to be the head of Katherine Harrison, who was lately imprisoned upon suspicion of witchcraft. Mary saw it walk to & fro in the chamber and went to her father's bedside then came back and disappeared. That day seven night next after, lying in her bed something came upon her in like manner as is formerly related, first on her legs & feet & then on her stomach, crushing & oppressing her very sore. She put forth her hand to feel (because there was no light in the room so as clearly to discern). Mary aforesaid felt a face, which she judged to be a woman's face, presently then she had a great blow on her fingers which pained her 2 days after, which she complained of to her father & mother, & made her fingers black and blue. During the former passages Mary called to her father & mother but could not wake them till it was gone. After this, the day of December in the night, (the night being very windy) something came again and spoke thus to her, saying to Mary aforesaid, You said that I would not come again, but are you not afraid of me. Mary said, No. The voice replied I will make you afraid before I have done with you; and then presently Mary was crushed & oppressed very much. Then Mary called often to her father and mother, they lying very near. Then the voice said, Though you do call they shall not hear till I am gone. Then the voice said, You said that I preserved my cart to carry me to the gallows, but I will make it a dear cart to you (which said words Mary remembered she had only spoke in private to her sister a little before & to no other.) Mary replied she feared her not, because God had kept her & would keep her still. The voice said she had a commission to kill her. Mary asked, Who gave you the commission? The voice replied God gave me the commission. Mary replied, The Devil is a liar from the beginning for God will not give commission to murder, therefore it must be from the devil. Then Mary was again pressed very much. Then the voice said, You will make known these things abroad when I am gone, but if you will promise me to keep these aforesaid matters secret I will come no more to afflict you. Mary replied I will tell it abroad. Whereas the said Mary mentions divers times in this former writing that she heard a voice, this said Mary affirmeth that she did & doth know that it was the voice of Katherine Harrison aforesaid; and

Mary aforesaid affirmeth that the substance of the whole relation is truth." Sworn in Court May 25, 1669. Attest John Allyn, Sec'y.

Elizabeth Smith—*Neighborly criticism—Fortune telling—Spinning yarn*

"Elizabeth the wife of Simon Smith of Thirty Mile Island testified that Catherine was noted by her and the rest of the family to be a great or notorious liar, a sabbath breaker, and one that told fortunes, and told the said Elizabeth her fortune, that her husband's name should be Simon; & also told the said Elizabeth some other matters that did come to pass; and also would oft speak and boast of her great familiarity with Mr. Lilley, one that told fortunes and foretold many matters that in furture times were to be accomplished. And also the said Katherine did often spin so great a quantity of fine linen yarn as the said Elizabeth did never know nor hear of any other woman that could spin so much. And further, the said Elizabeth said that Capt. Cullick observing the evil conversation in word and deed of the said Katherine turned her out of his service, one reason was because the said Katherine told fortunes." Taken upon oath Sept. 23, 1668 before John Allyn, Assistant.

On such evidence, October 12, 1669, the jury being called to give in their verdict upon the indictment of Katherine Harrison, returned that they find the prisoner guilty of the indictment.

But meanwhile important things in the history of the case had come to pass. Serious doubts arose in the minds of the magistrates as to accepting the verdict, and in their dilemma they took counsel not only of the law but of the gospel, and presented a series of questions to certain ministers—the same expedient adopted by the court at Salem twenty-three years later.

The answer of the ministers is in the handwriting of Rev. Gershom Bulkeley of Wethersfield, the author of the unique treatise *Will and Doom*. It was a remarkable paper as to preternatural apparitions, the character of evidence for conviction, and its cautions as to its acceptance. It was this:

"The answer of some ministers to the questions pr-pounded to them by the Honored Magistrates, Octobr 20, 1669. To ye 1st Quest whether a plurality of witnesses be necessary, legally to evidence one and ye same individual fact? Wee answer."

"That if the proofe of the fact do depend wholly upon testimony, there is then a necessity of a plurality of witnesses, to testify to one & ye same individual fact; & without such a plurality, there can be no legall evidence of it. Jno 8, 17. The testimony of two men is true; that is legally true, or the truth of order. & this Cht alledges to vindicate ye sufficiency of the testimony given to prove that individual facte, that he himselfe was ye Messias or Light of the World. Mat. 26, 59, 60."

"To the 2nd quest. Whether the preternatural apparitions of a person legally proved, be a demonstration of familiarity with ye devill? Wee anser, that it is not the pleasure of ye Most High, to suffer the wicked one to make an undistinguishable representation of any innocent person in a way of doing mischiefe, before a plurality of witnesses. The reason is because, this would utterly evacuate all human testimony; no man could testify, that he saw this pson do this or that thing, for it might be said, that it was ye devill in his shape."

"To the 3d & 4th quests together: Whether a vitious pson foretelling some future event, or revealing of a secret, be a demonstration of familiarity with the devill? Wee say thus much."

"That those things, whither past, present or to come, which are indeed secret, that is, cannot be knowne by human skill in arts, or strength of reason arguing from ye corse of nature, nor are made knowne by divine revelation either mediate or immediate, nor by information from man, must needes be knowne (if at all) by information from ye devill: & hence the comunication of such things, in way of divination (the pson prtending the certaine knowledge of them) seemes to us, to argue familiarity with ye devill, in as much as such a pson doth thereby declare his receiving the devills testimony, & yeeld up himselfe as ye devills instrument to comunicate the same to others."

And meanwhile Katherine herself had not been idle even in durance. With a dignity becoming such a communication, and in a desperate hope that justice and mercy might be meted out to her, she addressed a petition to the court setting forth with unconscious pathos some of the wrongs and sufferings she had endured in person and estate; and one may well understand why under such great provocation she told Michael Griswold that he would hang her though he damned a thousand souls, and as for his own soul it was damned long ago. Vigorous and emphatic words, for which perhaps Katherine was punished enough, as she was adjudged to pay Michael in two actions for slander, £25 and costs in one and £15 and costs in the other.

This was Katherine's appeal:

Filed: Wid. Harrisons greuances presented to the court 6th of Octobr 1669.

"A complaint of severall greiuances of the widow Harrisons which she desires the honored court to take cognizance of and as far as maybe to give her reliefe in."

"May it please this honored court, to have patience with mee a little: having none to complain to but the Fathers of the Commonweale; and yet meetting with many injurys, which necessitate mee to look out for some releeife. I am told to present you with these few lines, as a relation of the wrongs that I suffer, humbly crauing your serious consideration of my state a widdow; of my wrongs, (wch I conceive are great) and that as far as the rules of justice and equitie will allow, I may have right and a due recompence."

"That that I would present to you in the first place is we had a yoke of oxen one of wch spoyled at our stile before our doore, with blows upon the backe and side, so bruised that he was altogether unserviceable; about a fortnight or three weeks after the former, we had a cow spoyled, her back broke and two of her ribs, nextly I had a heifer in my barne yard, my ear mark of wch was cutt out and other ear marks set on; nextly I had a sow that had young pigs ear marked (in the stie) after the same manner; nextly I had a cow at the side of my yard, her jaw bone broke and one of her hoofs and a hole bored in her side, nextly I had a three yeare old heifer in the meadow stuck with knife or some weapon and wounded to death; nextly I had a cow in the street wounded in the bag as she stood before my door, in the street, nextly I had a sow went out into the woods, came home with ears luged and one of her hind legs cutt offe, lastly my corne in Mile Meadow much damnified with horses, they being staked upon it; it was wheat; All wch injurys, as they do sauor of enemy so I hope they will be looked upon by this honored court according to their natuer and judged according to there demerit, that so your poor suppliant may find some redrese; who is bold to subscribe."

"Your servant and supplyant, "KATHERINE HARRISON.

"Postscript. I had my horse wounded in the night, as he was in my pasture no creature save thre calves with him: More I had one two yeare old steer the back of it broke, in the barne yard, more I had a matter of 30 poles of hops cutt and spoyled; all wch things have hapened since my husband death, wch was last August was two yeare. There is wittnes to the oxen Jonathan & Josiah Gillert; to the cows being spoyled, Enoch Buck, Josiah Gilbert; to the cow that had her jaw bone broke, Dan, Rose, John, Bronson: to the heifer, one of widdow Stodder sons, and Willia Taylor; to the corne John Beckly; to the wound of the horse Anthony Wright, Goodman Higby; to the hops cutting, Goodwife Standish and Mary Wright; wch things being added, and left to your serious consideration, I make bold again to subscribe.

"Yours, "KATHERINE HARRISON."

At a special court of assistants held May 20, 1670, to which the General Assembly had referred the matter with power, the court having considered the verdict of the jury could not concur with them so as to sentence her to death, but dismissed her from her imprisonment, she paying her just fees; willing her to mind the fulfilment of removing from Wethersfield, "which is that will tend most to her own safety & the contentment of the people who are her neighbors."

In the same year, having paid the expenses of her trials and imprisonment, she removed to Westchester, New York. Being under suspicion of witchcraft, her presence was unwelcome to the inhabitants there and complaint was made to Governor Lovelace. She gave security for her civil carriage and good behavior, and at the General Court of Assizes held in New York in October, 1670, in the case of Katherine Harrison, widow, who was bound to the good behavior upon complaint of some of the inhabitants of Westchester, it was ordered, "that in regard there is nothing appears against her deserving the continuance of that obligation she is to be released from it, & hath liberty to remain in the town of Westchester where she now resides, or anywhere else in the government during her pleasure."

CHAPTER VII

"Although our fathers cannot be charged with having regarded the Devil in his respectful and deferential light, it must be acknowledged, that they gave him a conspicuous and distinguished—we might almost say a dignified—agency in the affairs of life and the government of the world: they were prone to confess, if not to revere, his presence, in all scenes and at all times. He occupied a wide space, not merely in their theology and philosophy, but in their daily and familiar thoughts." UPHAM'S *Salem Witchcraft*.

"There are in every community those who for one cause or another unfortunately incur the dislike and suspicion of the neighbors, and when belief in witchcraft prevailed such persons were easily believed to have familiarity with the evil one." *A Case of Witchcraft in Hartford* (Connecticut Magazine, November, 1899), HOADLEY.

Witchcraft in the Connecticut towns reached its climax in 1692—the fateful year at Salem, Massachusetts—and the chief center of its activity was in the border settlements at Fairfield. There, several women early in the year were accused of the crime, and among them Mercy Disborough. The testimonies against her were unique, and yet so typical that they are given in part as the second illustration.

MERCY (DISBRO) DISBOROUGH

A special court, presided over by Robert Treat, Governor, was held at Fairfield by order of the General Court, to try the witch cases, and September 14, 1692, a true bill was exhibited against Mercy Disborough, wife of Thomas Disborough of Compo in Fairfield, in these words:

"Mercy Disborough is complayned of & accused as guilty of witchcraft for that on the 25t of Aprill 1692 & in the 4th year of their Maties reigne & at sundry other times she hath by the instigation & help of the diuill in a preternaturall way afflicted & don harme to the bodyes & estates of sundry of their Maties subjects or to some of them contrary to the law of God, the peace of our soueraigne lord & lady the King & Queen their crowne & dignity."

"BILLA VERA."

Others were indicted and tried, at this session of the court and its adjournments, notably Elizabeth Clawson. Many depositions were taken in Fairfield and elsewhere, some of the defendants were discharged and others convicted, but Mercy Disborough's case was the most noted one in the tests applied, and in the conclusions to which it led. The whole case with its singular incidents is worthy of careful study. Some of the testimony is given here.

EDWARD JESOP—*The roast pig* – "*The place of Scripture*" – *The bewitched "cannoe"* – *The old cart horse* – *Optical illusions*

"Edward Jesop aged about 29 years testifieth that being at The: Disburrows house at Compoh sometime in ye beginning of last winter in ye evening he asked me to tarry & sup with him, & their I saw a pigg roasting that looked verry well, but when it came to ye table (where we had a very good lite) it seemed to me to have no skin upon it & looked very strangly, but when ye sd Disburrow began to cut it ye skin (to my apprehension) came againe upon it, & it seemed to be as it was when upon ye spit, at which strange alteration of ye pig I was much concerned however fearing to displease his wife by refusing to eat, I did eat some of ye pig, & at ye same time Isaac Sherwood being there & Disburrows wife & hee discoursing concerning a certain place of scripture, & I being of ye same mind that Sherwood was concerning yt place of scripture & Sherwood telling her where ye place was she brought a bible (that was of very large print) to me to read ye particular scripture, but tho I had a good light & looked ernestly upon ye book I could not see one letter but looking upon it againe when in her hand after she had turned over a few leaves I could see to read it above a yard of. Ye same night going home & coming to Compoh it seemed to be high water whereupon I went to a cannoe that was about ten rods of (which lay upon such a bank as ordinarily I could have shoved it into ye creek with ease) & though I lifted with all my might & lifted one end very high from ye ground I could by no means push it into ye creek & then ye water seemed to be so loe yt I might ride over, whereupon I went againe to ye water side but then it appeared as at first very high & then going to ye cannoe againe & finding that I could not get it into ye creek I thought to ride round where I had often been & knew ye way as well as before my own dore & had my old cart hors yet I could not keep him in ye road do what I could but he often turned aside into ye bushes and then went backwards so that tho I keep upon my hors & did my best indeauour to get home I was ye greatest part of ye night wandering before I got home altho I was not much more than two miles."

"Fairfield Septembr 15th 1692.

"Sworn in Court Septr 15 1692. Attests John Allyn, Secry."

JOHN BARLOW—*Mesmeric influence—Light and darkness—The falling out*

"John Barlow eaged 24 years or thairabout saieth and sd testifieth that soumtime this last year that as I was in bedd in the hous that Mead Jesuop then liuied in that Marsey Desbory came to me and layed hold on my fett and pinshed them (and) looked wishley in my feass and I strouff to rise and cold not and too speek and cold not. All the time that she was with me it was light as day as it semed to me—but when shee uanicht it was darck and I arose and hade a paine in my feet and leags some time after an our or too it remained.

Sometime before this aforesd Marcey and I had a falling out and shee sayed that if shee had but strength shee would teer me in peses."

"Sworn in court Septr 19, 92. Attests John Allyn."

BENJAMIN DUNING—"*Cast into ye watter*" – *Vindication of innocence – Mercy not to be hanged alone*

"A Speciall Cort held in Fairfield this 2d of June 1692.

"Marcy Disbrow ye wife of Thomas Disbrow of Fairfield was sometimes lately accused by Catren Branch servant to Daniell Wescoat off tormenting her whereupon sd Mercy being sent for to Stanford and ther examined upon suspecion of witchcraft before athaurity and fro thnce conueyed to ye county jaile and sd Mercy ernestly desireing to be tryed by being cast into ye watter yesterday wch was done this day being examind what speciall reason she had to be so desiring of such a triall her answer was yt it was to vindicate her innocency allso she sd Mercy being asked if she did not say since she was duckt yt if she was hanged shee would not be hanged alone her answer was yt she did say to Benje Duning do you think yt I would be such a fooll as to be hanged allone. Sd Benj. Duning aged aboue sixteen years testifies yt he heard sd Mercy say yesterday that if she was hanged she would not be hanged allone wch was sd upon her being urged to bring out others that wear suspected for wiches."

"Sept 15 1692 Sworn in Court by Benj. Duning attest John Allyn Secy

"Joseph Stirg aged about 38 declares that he wth Benj. Duning being at prison discoursing with the prisoner now at the bar he heard her say if she were hanged she would not be hanged alone. He tould her she implicitly owned herself a witch."

"Sworn in Court Sept. 15, atests John Allyn, Secry."

THOMAS HALLIBERCH—*A poor creature "damd" – Torment – A lost soul – Divination*

"Thomas Halliberch ye jayle keeper aged 41 testifieth and saith yt this morning ye date aboue Samull Smith junr. came to his house and sad somthing to his wife somthing concerning Mercy and his wifes answer was Oh poor creature upon yt Mercy mad answer & sd poor creature indeed & sd shee had been tormented all night. Sd Halliberch answered her yt it was ye devill her answer was she did beleue it was and allso yt she sed to it in ye name of ye Father Son and Holy Gost also sd Halliberch saith yt sd Mercy sd that her soul was damd for yesterdays worke. Mercy owned before this court yt she did say to sd Halliberch that it was reuealled to her yt shee wisht she had not damd her soule for yesterdays work and also sad before this cort she belieued that there was a deuination in all her trouble."

"Owned by the prisoner in court Sept. 15, 1692. attest John Allyn, Secy"

THOMAS BENIT, ELIZABETH BENIT—*"A birds taile" – A family difference – "Ye Scripture words" – The lost "calues and lams"*

"Thos. Benit aged aboute 50 yrs testifieth yt Mercy Disbrow tould him yt shee would make him as bare as a birds taile, which he saith was about two or three yrs sine wch was before he lost any of his creatures."

"Elizabeth Benit aged about 20 yrs testifieth yt Mercy Disbrow did say that it should be prest heeped and running ouer to her sd Elizabth; wch was somtime last winter after som difference yt was aboute a sow of Benje. Rumseyes."

"Mercy Disbrow owns yt she did say those words to sd Elizabeth & yt she did tell her yt it was ye scripture words & named ye place of scripture which was about a day after."

"The abousd Thos. Benit saith yt after ye sd Mercy had expressed herself as above, he lost a couple of two yr old calues in a creek running by Halls Islande, which catle he followed by ye track &

founde them one against a coue of ice & ye other about high water marke, & yt they went into ye creek som distance from ye road where ye other catle went not, & also yt he lost 30 lams wthin about a fortnights time after ye sd two catle died som of sd lams about a week old & som a fortnight & in good liueing case & allso saith yt som time after ye sd lams died he lost two calues yt he fectht up ouer night & seemed to be well & wear dead before ye next morning one of them about a fortnight old ye one a sucker & ye other not."

HENRY GREY—*The roaring calfe—The mired cow—The heifer and cart whip—Hard words—"Creeses in ye cetle"*

"The said Henry saith yt aboute a year agou or somthing more yt he had a calfe very strangly taken and acted things yt are very unwonted, it roared very strangly for ye space of near six or seven howers & allso scowered extraordinarily all which after an unwonted maner; & also saith he had a lame after a very strange maner it being well and ded in about an houre and when it was skined it lookt as if it had been bruised or pinched on ye shoulders and allso saith yt about two or three months agou he and Thos Disbrow & sd Disbroughs wife was makeing a bargaine about a cetle yt sd Henry was to haue & had of sd Disbrough so in time they not agreeing sd Henry carried ye cetle to them againe & then sd Dibroughs wife was very angry and many hard words pased & yt som time since about two months he lost a cow which was mired in a swampe and was hanged by one leg in mire op to ye gambrill and her nose in the water and sd cow was in good case & saith he had as he judged about 8 pound of tallow out of sd cow & allso yt he had a thre yr old heifer came home about three weeks since & seemed to ale somthing she lay downe & would haue cast herself but he pruented her & he cut a piece of her eare & still shee seemed to be allmost dead & then he sent for his cart whip & gave ye cow a stroak wth it & she arose suddenly and ran from him & he followed her & struck her sundry times and yt wthin about one hour he judges she was well & chewed her cud allso sd Henry saith yt ye ketle he had of sd Disbrow loockt like a new ketle the hamer stroakes and creeses was plaine to be seen in ye cetle, from ye time he had it untill a short time before he carried it home & then in about a quarter of an hour, the cetle changed its looks & seemed to be an old cetle yt had been used about 20 years and yt sundry nailes appeared which he could not see before and allso saith yt somtime lately he being at his brother Jacob Grays house & Mercy Disbrough being there she begane to descorse about ye kitle yt because he would not haue ye cetle shee had said that it should cost him two cows which he tould her he could prove she had sed & her answer was Aye: & then was silent, & he went home & when he com home he heard Thomas Benit say he had a cow strangly taken yt day & he sent for his cart whip & whipye cow & shee was soon well againe & as near as he could com at it was about ye same time yt he tould Mercy he could prove what shee sad about ye two cows and allso saith yt as soon as he came home ye same time his wife tould him yt while Thos Benit had ye cart whip one of sd Henrys calues was taken strangly & yt she sent for ye whip & before ye whip came ye calf was well."

JOHN GRUMMON—*A sick child—Its unbewitching—Benit's threats—Mercy's tenderness*

"John Grummon senr saith yt about six year agou he being at Compo with his wife & child & ye child being very well as to ye outward vew and it being suddenly taken very ill & so remained a little while upon wch he being much troubled went out & heard young Thomas Benit threaten Mercy Disbrow & bad her unbewitch his uncles child whereupon she came ouer to ye child & ye child was well.

"Thomas Benit junr aged 27 years testifieth yt at ye same time of ye above sd childs illness he came into ye house wher it was & he spoke to sd John Gruman to go & scould at Mercy & tould him if he sd Gruman would not he would wherupon he sd Benit went out and called to Mercy & bad her come and unbewitch his unkle Grumans child or else he would beat her hart out then sd mercy imediatly came ouer and stroaked ye child & sd God forbad she should hurt ye child and imediately after ye child was well."

ANN GODFREE—*The frisky oxen – Neighborly interest – The "beer out of ye barrill" – Mixed theology – The onbewitched sow*

"Ann Godfree aged 27 years testifieth yt she came to Thos Disbrows house ye next morning after it was sd yt Henry Grey whipt his cow and sd Disbrows wife lay on ye bed & stretcht out her arme & sd to her oh! Ann I am allmost kild; & further saith yt about a year & eleven months agou she went to sd Disbrows house wth young Thos Benits wife & told Mercy Disbrow yt Henry Greys wife sed she had bewitcht his her husbands oxen & made y jump ouer ye fence & made ye beer jump out of ye barrill & Mercy answered yt there was a woman came to her & reuiled her & asked what shee was doing she told her she was praying to her God, then she asked her who was her god allso tould her yt her god was ye deuill; & Mercy said she bad ye woman go home & pray to her god & she went home but shee knew not whether she did pray or not; but she sed God had met wth her for she had died a hard death for reuileing on her & yt when ye sd Thos Benits wife & she came away sd Benits wife tould her yt woman yt was spoaken of was her sister and allso sed yt shee had heard those words which Mercy had related to her pas between Mercy and her sister. Upon yt sd An saith she would haue gon back & haue talked againe to Mercy & Thomas Benit senr bad her she should not for she would do her som mischief and yt night following shee sd Ann saith she could not sleep & shee heard a noyse about ye house & allso heard a noyse like as tho a beast wear knoct with an axe & in ye morning their was a heifer of theirs lay ded near ye door. Allso sd An saith yt last summer she had a sow very sick and sd Mercy cam bye & she called to her & bad her on-bewitch her sow & tould her yt folks talked of ducking her but if she would not onbewitch her sow she should need no ducking & soon after yt her sow was well and eat her meat." That both what is on this side & the other is sworne in court.

"Sept 15, 92. Attests, John Allyn Secy"

"It has been heretofore noted that during her trial—from the records of which the foregoing testimony has been taken—the prisoner Mercy Disborough was subjected to a search for witch marks by a committee of women, faithfully sworn narrowly and truly to inspect and search. This indignity was repeated, and the women agreed "that there is found on her boddy as before they found, and nothing else." But the accused in order to her further detection was subjected to another test of English parentage, recommended by the authorities and embodied in the criminal codes. It was the notorious water test, or ordeal by water. September 15, 1692, this test was made, chiefly on the testimony of a young girl subject to epileptic fits and hysterics, who was carried into the meetinghouse where the examination was being held. Thus runs the record:

Daniel Westcott's "gerle" – Scenes in the meeting house – "Ye girl" – Mercy's voice – Usual paroxisme

"The afflicted person being carried into ye meeting house & Mercy Disbrow being under examination by ye honable court & whilst she was speaking ye girl came to her sences, & sd she heard Mercy Disbrow saying withall where is she, endeavoring to raise herself, with her masters help got almost up, in ye open view of present, & Mercy Disbrow looking about on her, she immediately fel down into a fit again. A 2d time she came to herself whilst in ye meeting house, & askd whers Mercy, I hear her voice, & with that turned about her head (she lying with her face from her) & lookd on her, then laying herself down in like posture as before sd tis she, Ime sure tis she, & presently fell into a like paroxisme or fit as she usually is troubled with."

Mercy Disborough, and another woman on trial at the same time (Elizabeth Clauson), were put to the test together, and two eyewitnesses of the sorry exhibition of cruelty and delusion made oath that they saw Mercy and Elizabeth bound hand and foot and put into the water, and that they swam upon the water like a cork, and when one labored to press them into the water they buoyed up like cork. [G]

[G] Depositions of Abram Adams and Jonathan Squire, September 15, 1692.

At the close of the trial the jury disagreed and the prisoner was committed "to the common goale there to be kept in safe custody till a return may be made to the General Court for further direction what shall be don in this matter;" and the gentlemen of the jury were also to be ready, when further called by direction of the General Court, to perfect their verdict. The General Court ordered the Special Court to meet again "to put an issue to those former matters."

October 28, 1692, this entry appears of record:

"The jury being called to make a return of their indictment that had been committed to them concerning Mercy Disborough, they return that they find the prisoner guilty according to the indictment of familiarity with Satan. The jury being sent forth upon a second consideration of their verdict returned that they saw no reason to alter their verdict, but to find her guilty as before. The court approved of their verdict and the Governor passed sentence of death upon her."

The hesitation of the jury to agree upon a verdict, the reference to the General Court for more specific authority to act, all point to serious question of the evidence, the motives of witnesses, the value of the traditional and lawful tests of the guilt of the accused.

In the search for facts which the old records certify to at this late day, one is deeply impressed by the wisdom and potency of the sober afterthought and conclusions of some of the clergy, lawyers, and men of affairs, who sat as judges and jurors in the witch trials, which led them to weigh and analyze the evidence, spectral and otherwise, and so call a halt in the prosecutions and convictions.

What some of the Massachusetts men did and said in the contemporaneous outbreak at Salem has been shown, but nowhere is the reaction there more clearly illustrated than in the statement of Reverend John Hale—great-grandsire of Nathan Hale, the revolutionary hero—the long time pastor at Beverly Farms, who from personal experience became convinced of the grave errors at the Salem trials, and in his *Modest Inquiry* in 1697 said:

"Such was the darkness of that day, the tortures and lamentations of the afflicted, and the power of former precedents, that we walked in the clouds and could not see our way.... observing the events of that sad catastrophe,—Anno 1692,—I was brought to a more strict scanning of the principles I had imbibed, and by scanning to question, and by questioning at length to reject many of them." *Nathan Hale* (p. 10), Johnston.

But no utterance takes higher rank, or deserves more consideration in its appeal to sanity, justice, and humanity, than the declaration of certain ministers and laymen of Connecticut, in giving their advice and "reasons" for a cessation of the prosecutions for witchcraft in the colonial courts, and for reprieving Mercy Disborough under sentence of death. This is the remarkable document:

"Filed: The ministers aduice about the witches in Fayrfield, 1692.

"As to ye evidences left to our consideration respecting ye two women suspected of witchcraft at Fairfield we offer

"1. That we cannot but give our concurrance with ye generallity of divines that ye endeavour of conviction of witchcraft by swimming is unlawful and sinfull & therefore it cannot afford any evidence.

"2. That ye unusuall excresencies found upon their bodies ought not to be allowed as evidence against them without ye approbation of some able physitians.

"3. Respecting ye evidence of ye afflicted maid we find some things testifyed carrying a suspition of her counterfeiting; Others that plainly intimate her trouble from ye mother which improved by craft may produce ye most of those strange & unusuall effects affirmed of her; & of those things that by some may be thought to be diabolical or effects of witchcraft. We apprehend her applying of them to these persons merely from ye appearance of their spectres to her to be very uncertain and failable from ye easy deception of her senses & subtile devices of ye devill, wherefore cannot think her a sufficient witnesse; yet we think that her affliction being something strange it well deserves a farther inquiry.

"4. As to ye other strange accidents as ye dying of cattle &c., we apprehend ye applying of them to these women as matters of witchcraft to be upon very slender & uncertain grounds.

"Hartford JOSEPH ELIOT "Octobr 1692 TIMOTHY WOOD-BRIDGE."

"The rest of ye ministers gave their approbation to ye sum of what is ... above written tho this could not be drawen up before their departure."

(Above in handwriting of Rev. Timothy Woodbridge.) "Filed: Reasons of Repreuing Mercy Desbrough.

"To the Honrd Gen: Assembly of Connecticut Colony sitting in Hartford. Reasons of repreuing Mercy Disbrough from being put to death until this Court had cognizance of her case.

"First, because wee that repreued her had power by the law so to do. Secondly, because we had and haue sattisfying reasons that the sentence of death passed against her ought not to be executed which reasons we give to this Court to be judge of

"1st. The jury that brought her in guilty (which uerdict was the ground of her condemnation) was not the same jury who were first charged with this prisoners deliuerance and who had it in charg many weeks. Mr. Knowles was on the jury first sworn to try this woman and he was at or about York when the Court sate the second time and when the uerdict was given, the jury was altered and another man sworn.

"It is so inuiolable a practice in law that the indiudual jurors and jury that is charged with the deliuerance of a prisoner in a capital case and on whom the prisoner puts himself or herself to be tryed must try it and they only that al the presidents in Old England and New confirm 9it and not euer heard of til this time to be inouated. And yet not only president but the nature of the thing inforces it for to these juors the law gaue this power vested it in them they had it in right of law and it is incompatible and impossible that it should be uested in these and in others too for then two juries may haue the same power in the same case one man altered the jury is altered.

"Tis the birthright of the Kings' subjects so and no otherwise to be tryed and they must not be despoyled of it.

"Due form of law is that alone wherein the ualidity of verdicts and judgments in such cases stands and if a real and apparent murtherer be condemned and executed out of due form of law it is inditable against them that do it for in such case the law is superseded by arbitrary doings.

"What the Court accepts and the prisoner accepts differing from the law is nothing what the law admitts is al in the case.

"If one jury may be changed two, ten, the whole may be so, and solemn oathe made uain.

"Wee durst not but dissent from and declare against such alterations by our repreueing therefore the said prisoner when ye were informed of this business about her jury, and we pray this honored Court to take heed what they do in it now it is roled to their doore and that at least they be well sattisfied from able lawyers that such a chang is in law alowable ere this prisoner be executed least they bring themselues into inextricable troubles and the whole country. Blood is a great thing and we cannot but open our mouths for the dumb in the cause of one appointed to die by such a uerdict.

"2dly. We had a good accompt of the euidences giuen against her that none of them amounted to what Mr. Perkins, Mr. Bernard and Mr. Mather with others state as sufficiently conuictiue of witchcraft, namely 1st Confession (this there was none of) 2dly two good wittnesses proueing som act or acts done by the person which could not be but by help of the deuill, this is the summe of what they center in as thair books show as for the common things of spectral euidence il euents after quarels or threates, teates, water tryalls and the like with suspitious words they are al discarded and som of them abominated by the most judicious as to be conuictiue of witchcraft and the miserable toyl they are in the Bay for adhereing to these last mentioned litigious things is warning enof, those that will make witchcraft of such things will make hanging work apace and we are informed of no other but such as these brought against this woman.

"These in brief are our reasons for repreueing this prisoner. May 12th, 1693. SAMUELL WILLIS. WM PITKIN NATH STANLY.

"The Court may please to consider also how farr these proceedings do put a difficulty on any further tryal of this woman."

All honor to Joseph Elliot, Timothy Woodbridge and their ministerial associates; to Samuel Willis, Pitkin and Nath. Stanly, level-headed men of affairs, all friends of the court called upon for advice and counsel—who gave it in full scriptural measure. [H]

[H] Mercy Disborough was pardoned, as the records show that she was living in 1707.

CHAPTER VIII

"Old Matthew Maule was executed for the crime of witchcraft. He was one of the martyrs to that terrible delusion, which should teach us, among its other morals, that the influential classes, and those who take upon themselves to be leaders of the people, are fully liable to all the passionate error that has ever characterized the maddest mob."

"Clergymen, judges, statesmen—the wisest, calmest, holiest persons of their day—stood in the inner circle round about the gallows, loudest to applaud the work of blood, latest to confess themselves miserably deceived."

"This old reprobate was one of the sufferers when Cotton Mather, and his brother ministers, and the learned judges, and other wise men, and Sir William Phipps, the sagacious governor, made such laudable efforts to weaken the great enemy of souls by sending a multitude of his adherents up the rocky pathway of Gallows Hill." *The House of the Seven Gables* (20: 225), HAWTHORNE.

"Then, too, the belief in witchcraft was general. Striking coincidences, personal eccentricities, unusual events and mysterious diseases seemed to find an easy explanation in an unholy compact with the devil. A witticism attributed to Judge Sewall, one of the judges in these trials, may help us to understand the common panic: 'We know who's who but not which is witch.' That was the difficulty. At a time when every one believed in witchcraft it was easy to suspect one's neighbor. It was a characteristic superstition of the century and should be classed with the barbarous punishments and religious intolerance of the age." *N.E. Hist. Towns.*—LATIMER'S—*Salem* (150).

Multiplication of these witchcraft testimonies, quaint and curious, vulgar and commonplace, evil and pathetic, voices all of a strange superstition, understandable only as through them alone can one gain a clear perspective of the spirit of the time and place, would prove wearisome. They may well remain in the ancient records until they find publicity in detail in some accurate and complete history of the beginnings of the commonwealth—including this strange chapter in its unique history.

It will, however, serve a present necessary purpose, and lead to a more exact conception of the reign of unreason, if glimpses be taken here and there of a few of the statements made on oath in some of the other cases.

ELIZABETH SEAGER

Daniell Gabbett and Margaret Garrett—*The mess of parsnips—Hains' "hodg podg"—Satan's interference*

"The testimony of Daniell Garrett senior and the testimony of Margarett Garrett. Goodwife Gaarrett saith that goodwife Seager said there was a day kept at Mr. Willis in reference to An Coale; and she further said she was in great trouble euen in agony of spirit, the ground as follows that she sent her owne daughtr Eliza Seager to goodwife Hosmer to carry her a mess a parsnips. Goodwife Hosmer was not home. She was at Mr. Willis at the fast. Goodm Hosmer and his son was at home. Goodm Hosmer bid the child carry the parsnips home againe he would not receiue them and if her mother desired a reason, bid her send her father and he would tell him the reason. Goodwife Seager upon the return of the parsnips was much troubled and sent for her husband and sent him up to Goodm Hosmer to know the reason why he would not reciue the parsnips, and he told goodman Seager it was because An Coale at the fast at Mr. Willis cryed out against his wife as being a witch and he would not receiue the parsnips least he should be brought in hereaftr as a testimony against his wife. Then goodwif Seager sd that Mr. Hains had writt a great deal of hodg podg that An Coale had sd that she was under suspicion for a witch, and then she went to prayer, and did adventure to bid Satan go and tell them she was no witch. This deponent after she had a little paused said, who did you say, then goodw Seger sd againe she had sent Satan to tell them she was no witch. This deponent asked her why she made use of Satan to tell them, why she did not besech God to tell them she was no witch. She answered because Satan knew she was no witch. Goodman Garrett testifies that before him and his wife, Goodwife Seager said that she sent Satan to tell them she was no witch."

ROBERT STERNE, STEPHEN HART, JOSIAH WILLARD AND DANIEL PRATT—*Four women – Two black creatures – A kettle and a dance – "That place in the Acts about the 7 sons"*

"Robert Sterne testifieth as followeth.

"I saw this woman goodwife Seager in ye woods wth three more women and with them I saw two black creaures like two Indians but taller. I saw likewise a kettle there over a fire. I saw the women dance round these black creatures and whiles I looked upon them one of the women G: Greensmith said looke who is yonder and then they ran away up the hill. I stood still and ye black things came towards mee and then I turned to come away. He further saith I knew the psons by their habits or clothes haueing observed such clothes on them not long before."

"Wee underwritten do testifie, that goodwife Seager said, (upon the relateing of goodwife Garrett testimony, in reference to Seager sending Satan,) that the reason why she sent Satan, was because he knew she was no witch, we say Seager said Dame you can remember part of what I said, but you do not speak of the whole you say nothing of what I brought to prove that Satan knew that I was no witch. I brought that place in the Acts, about the 7 sons that spake to the euill spirits in the name of Jesus whom Paul preacheth I have forgot there names.

"STEPHEN HART "JOSIAH WILLARD "DANIEL PRATT."

MRS. MIGAT—*A warm greeting, "how doe yow" – "god was naught" – "Hell need not be feared, for she should not burn in ye fire" – The ghost "stracke"*

"Mrs. Migat sayth she went out to give her calues meat, about fiue weekes since, & goodwif Segr came to her and shaked her by ye arme, & sd she how doe yow, how doe yow, Mrs. Migatt.

"2d Mrs. Migatt alsoe saith: a second time goodwife Segr came her towerds ye little riuer, a litle below ye house wch she now dweleth in, and told her, that god was naught, god was naught, it was uery good to be a witch and desired her to be one, she should not ned fare going to hell, for she should not burne in ye fire Mrs. Migat said to her at this time that she did not loue her; she was very naught, and goodwif Segr shaked her by ye hands and bid her farwell, and desired her, not to tell any body what shee had said unto her.

"3d Time. Mrs. Migat affirmeth yt goodwife Segr came to her at ye hedge corner belonging to their house lot, and their spake to her but what she could not tell, wch caused Mrs. Migatt (as she sayth) to (turn) away wth great feare.

"Mrs. Migat sayth a little before ye floud this spring, goodwife Segr came into thaire house, on a mone shining night, and took her by ye hand and stracke her on ye face as she was in beed wth her husband, whome she could wake, and then goodwife Segr went away, and Mrs. Migat went to ye dore but darst not looke out after her.

"These pticulers Mrs. Migat charged goodwife Segr wth being face to face, at Mr. Migats now dwelling house."

"John Talcott."

Staggerings of the jury – "Shuffing" – "Grinding teeth" – Seager's denials – Contradictions – Acquittal

"Janur 16 1662

"The causes why half the jury ore more did in their vote cast gooddy Seger (and the rest of the jury were deeply suspitious, and were at a great loss and staggeringe whereby they were sometimes likely to com up in their judgments to the rest, whereby she was allmost gone and cast as the foreman expressed to her at giuing in of the verdict) are these

"First it did apeare by legall euidence that she had intimat familliarity with such as had been wiches, viz goody Sanford and goody Ayrs. 2ly this she did in open court stoutly denie saing the witnesses were preiudiced persons, and that she had now more intimacy then they themselves, and when the witneses questioned with her about frequent being there she said she went to lerne to knitt; this also she stoutly denied, and said of the witneses they belie me, then when Mr. John Allen sd did she not teach you to knitt, she answered sturdily and sayd, I do not know that I am bound to tell you & at another time being pressed to answ she sayd, nay I will hould what I have if I must die, yet after this she confessed that she had so much intimacy with one of ym as that they did change woorke one with another. 3ly she having sd that she did hate goody Aiers it did appear that she bore her great yea more than ordinarily good will as apeared by releeuing her in her truble, and was couert way, and was trubled that is was discouered; likewise when goody Aiers said in court, this will take away my liffe, goody Seger shuffed her with her hand & sd hould your tongue wt grinding teeth Mr. John Allen being one wittnes hearto when he had spoken, she sd they seek my innocent blood; the magistrats replied, who she sd euery body. 4ly being spoken to about triall by swiming, she sagd the diuill that caused me to com heare can keep me up.

"About the buisnes of fliing the most part thought it was not legally proued.

"Lastly the woman and Robert Stern being boath upon oath their wittnes was judged legall testimony ore evidence only som in the jury because Sternes first words upon his oath were, I saw these women and as I take it goody Seger was there though after that he sayd, I saw her there, I knew her well I know God will require her blood at my hands if I should testifie falsly. Allso bec he sd he saw her kittle, there being at so great a distance, they doubted that these things did not only weaken & blemish his testimony, but also in a great measure disable it for standing to take away liffe."

"WALT. FYLER."

Elizabeth Seager was acquitted.

ELIZABETH GODMAN

Of all the women who set the communities ablaze with their witcheries, none in fertility of invention and performance surpassed Elizabeth Godman of New Haven—a member of the household of Stephen Goodyear, the Deputy Governor. Reverend John Davenport said, in a sermon of the time, "that a froward discontented frame of spirit was a subject fitt for ye Devill," and Elizabeth was accused by Goodwife Larremore and others of being in "such a frame of spirit," and of practicing the black arts.

She promptly haled her accusers before a court of magistrates, August 4, 1653, with Governor Theophilus Eaton and Deputy Governor Stephen Goodyear present; and when asked what she charged them with, she desired that "a wrighting might be read—wch was taken in way of examination before ye magistrate," in May, 1653. The "wrighting" did not prove helpful to Elizabeth's case. The statements of witnesses and of the accused are in some respects unique, and of a decided personal quality.

"Hobbamocke" – The "swonding fitt" – Lying – Evil communications – The Indian's statement – "Ye boyes sickness" – "Verey strang fitts" – "Figgs" – "Pease porridge" – "A sweate" – Mrs. Goodyeare's opinion – Absorption – Contradictions – Goodwife Thorp's chickens – "Water and wormes"

"Mris. Godman was told she hath warned to the court diuers psons, vizd: Mr. Goodyeare, Mris. Goodyeare, Mr. Hooke, Mris. Hooke, Mris. Atwater, Hanah & Elizabeth Lamberton, goodwife Larremore, goodwife Thorpe, &c., and was asked what she had to charge them wth, she said they had given out speeches that made folkes thinke she was a witch, and first she charged Mris. Atwater to be ye cause of all, and to cleere things desired a wrighting might be read wch was taken in way of examination before ye magistrate, (and in here after entred,) wherein sundrie things concerning Mris. Atwater is specifyed wch we now more fully spoken to, and she further said that Mris. Atwater had said that she thought she was a witch and that Hobbamocke was her husband, but could proue nothing, though she was told that she was beforehand warned to prepare her witnesses ready, wch she hath not done, if she haue any. After sundrie of the passages in ye wrighting were read, she was asked if these things did not giue just ground of suspition to all that heard them that she was a witch. She confessed they did, but said if she spake such things as is in Mr. Hookes relation she was not herselfe.... Beside what is in the papr, Mris. Godman was remembred of a passage spoken of at the gouernors aboute Mr. Goodyeare's falling into a swonding fitt after hee had spoken something one night in the exposition of a chapter, wch she (being present) liked not but said it was against her, and as soone as Mr. Goodyeare had done duties she flung out of the roome in a discontented way and cast a fierce looke vpon Mr. Goodyeare as she went out, and imediately Mr. Goodyeare (though well before) fell into a swond, and beside her notorious lying in this buisnes, for being asked how she came to know this, she said she was present, yet Mr. Goodyeare, Mris. Goodyeare, Hanah and Elizabeth Lamberton all affirme she was not in ye roome but gone vp into the chamber."

THE "WRIGHTING"

"The examination of Elizabeth Godman, May 12th, 1653.

"Elizabeth Godman made complainte of Mr. Goodyeare, Mris. Goodyeare, Mr. Hooke, Mris. Hooke, Mris. Bishop, Mris. Atwater, Hanah & Elizabeth Lamberton, and Mary Miles, Mris. Atwaters maide, that they haue suspected her for a witch; she was now asked what she had against Mr. Hooke and Mris. Hooke; she said she heard they had something against her aboute their soone. Mr. Hooke said hee was not wthout feares, and hee had reasons for it; first he said it wrought suspition in his minde because shee was shut out at Mr. Atwaters vpon suspition, and hee was troubled in his sleepe aboute witches when his boye, was sicke, wch was in a verey strang manner, and hee looked vpon her as a mallitious one, and prepared to that mischiefe, and she would be often speaking aboute witches and rather justifye them then condemne them; she said why doe they provoake them, why doe they not let them come into the church. Another time she was speaking of witches wthout any occasion giuen her, and said if they accused her for a witch she would haue them to the gouernor, she would trounce them. Another time she was saying she had some thoughts, what if the Devill should come to sucke her, and she resolued he should not sucke her.... Time, Mr. Hookes Indian, said in church meeting time she would goe out and come in againe and tell them what was done at meeting. Time asking her who told, she answered plainly she would not tell, then Time said did not ye Devill tell you.... Time said she heard her one time talking to herselfe, and she said to her, who talke you too, she said, to you; Time said you talke to ye Devill, but she made nothing of it. Mr. Hooke further said, that he hath heard that they that are adicted that way would hardly be kept away from ye houses where they doe mischiefe, and so it was wth her when his boy was sicke, she would not be kept away from him, nor gott away when she was there, and one time Mris. Hooke bid her goe away, and thrust her from ye boye, but she turned againe and said she would looke on him. Mris. Goodyeare said that one time she questioned wth Elizabeth Godmand aboute ye boyes sickness, and said what thinke you of him, is he not strangly handled, she replyed, what, doe you thinke hee is bewitched; Mris. Goodyeare said nay I will keepe my thoughts to myselfe, but in time God will discouer ...

"Mr. Hooke further said, that when Mr. Bishop was married, Mris. Godman came to his house much troubled, so as he thought it might be from some affection to him, and he asked her, she said yes; now it is suspitious that so soone as they were contracted Mris. Byshop fell into verey strang fitts wch hath continewed at times euer since, and much suspition there is that she hath bine the cause of the loss of Mris. Byshops chilldren, for she could tell when Mris. Bishop was to be brought to bedd, and hath giuen out that she kills her chilldren wth longing, because she longs for every thing she sees, wch Mris. Bishop denies.... Another thing suspitious is, that she could tell Mris. Atwater had figgs in her pocket when she saw none of them; to that she answered she smelt them, and could smell figgs if she came in the roome, nere them that had them; yet at this time Mris. Atwater had figgs in her pocket and came neere her, yet she smelt them not; also Mris. Atwater said that Mris. Godman could tell that they one time had pease porridge, when they could none of them tell how she came to know, and beeing asked she saith she see ym on the table, and another time she saith she was there in ye morning when the maide set them on. Further Mris. Atwater saith, that that night the figgs was spoken of they had strangers to supper, and Mris. Godman was at their house, she cutt a sopp and put in pann; Betty Brewster called the maide to tell her & said she was aboute her workes of darkness, and was suspitious of Mris. Godman, and spake to her of it, and that night Betty Brewster was in a most misserable case, heareing a most dreadfull noise wch put her in great feare and trembling, wch put her into such a sweate as she was all on a water when Mary Miles came to goe to bed, who had fallen into a sleepe by the fire wch vsed not to doe, and in ye morning she looked as one yt had bine allmost dead....

"Mris. Godman accused Mr. Goodyeare for calling her downe when Mris. Bishop was in a sore fitt, to looke vpon her, and said he doubted all was not well wth her, and that hee feared she was a witch, but Mr. Goodyeare denyed that; vpon this Mris. Godman was exceeding angrie and would haue the servants called to witnes, and bid George the Scochman goe aske his master who bewitched her for she was not well, and vpon this presently Hanah Lamberton (being in ye roome) fell into a verey sore fitt in a verey strang maner....

"Another time Mris. Goodyeare said to her, Mris. Elzebeth what thinke you of my daughters case; she replyed what, doe you thinke I haue bewitched her; Mris. Goodyeare said if you be the ptie looke to it, for they intend to haue such as is suspected before the magistrate.

"Mris. Godman charged Hanah Lamberton that she said she lay for somewhat to sucke her, when she came in hott one day and put of some cloathes and lay vpon the bed in her chamber. Hanah said she and her sister Elizabeth went vp into the garet aboue her roome, and looked downe & said, looke how she lies, she lyes as if som bodey was sucking her, & vpon that she arose and said, yes, yes, so there is; after said Hanah, she hath something there, for so there seemed as if something was vnder the cloathes; Elizabeth said what haue you there, she said nothing but the cloathes, and both Hanah & Eliza. say that Mris. Godman threatened Hanah, and said let her looke to it for God will bring it vpon her owne head, and about two dayes after, Hanahs fitts began, and one night especially had a dreadfull fitt, and was pinched, and heard a hedious noise, and was in a strang manner sweating and burning, and some time cold and full of paine yt she shriked out.

"Elizabeth Lamberton saith that one time ye chilldren came downe & said Mris. Godman was talking to herselfe and they were afraide, then she went vp softly and heard her talke, what, will you fetch me some beare, will you goe, will you goe, and ye like, and one morning aboute breake of day Henry Boutele said he heard her talke to herselfe, as if some body had laine wth her....

"Mris. Goodyeare said when Mr. Atwaters kinswoman was married Mris. Bishop was there, and the roome being hott she was something fainte, vpon that Mris. Godman said she would haue many of these fainting fitts after she was married, but she saith she remembers it not....

"Goodwife Thorp complained that Mris. Godman came to her house and asked to buy some chickens, she said she had none to sell, Mris. Godman said will you giue them all, so she went away, and she thought then that if this woman was naught as folkes suspect, may be she will smite my chickens, and quickly after one chicken dyed, and she remembred she had heard if they were bewitched they would consume wthin, and she opened it and it was consumed in ye gisard to water & wormes, and divers others of them droped, and now they are missing and it is likely dead, and she neuer saw either hen or chicken that was so consumed wthin wth wormes. Mris. Godman said goodwife Tichenor had a whole brood so, and Mris. Hooke had some so, but for Mris. Hookes it was contradicted presently. This goodwife Thorp thought good to declare that it may be considered wth other things."

The court decided that Elizabeth's carriage and confession rendered her "suspitious" of witchcraft, and admonished her that "if further proofe come these passages will not be forgotten."

The further proof came forth promptly, since in August, 1655, Elizabeth was again called before the court for witchcraft, and the witnesses certified to "the doing of strange things."

The Governor's quandary – Elizabeth's "spirituall armour" – "The jumbling at the chamber dore" – The lost grapes – The tethered calfe – "Hott beare"

"At a court held at Newhaven the 7th of August 1655.

"Elizabeth Godman was again called before the Court, and told that she lies under suspition for witchcraft, as she knowes, the grounds of which were examined in a former court, and by herselfe confessed to be just grounds of suspition, wch passages were now read, and to these some more are since added, wch are now to be declared.

"Mr. Goodyeare said that the last winter, upon occasion of Gods afflicting hand upon the plantation by sickness, the private meeting whereof he is had appointed to set a day apart to seeke God: Elizabeth Godman desired she might be there; he told her she was under suspition, and it would be offensive; she said she had great need of it, for she was exercised wth many temptations, and saw strange appearitions, and lights aboute her bed, and strange sights wch affrighted her; some of his family said if she was affraide they would worke wth her in the day and lye with her in the night, but she refused and was angry and said she would haue none to be wth her for she had her spirituall armour aboute her. She was asked the reason of this; she answered, she said so to Mr. Goodyeare, but it was her fancy troubled her, and she would haue none lye wth her because her bed was weake; she was told that might haue been mended; then she said she was not willing to haue any of them wth her, for if any thing had fallen ill wth them they would haue said that she had bine the cause."

Mr. Goodyeare further declared that aboute three weekes agoe he had a verey great disturbance in his family in the night (Eliza: Godman hauing bine the day before much discontented because Mr. Goodyeare warned her to provide another place to live in) his daughter Sellevant, Hanah Goodyeare, and Desire Lamberton lying together in the chamber under Eliza: Godman; after they were in bed they heard her walke up and downe and talk aloude; but could not tell what she said; then they heard her go downe the staires and come up againe; they fell asleep, but were after awakened wth a great jumbling at the chamber dore, and something came into the chamber wch jumbled at the other end of the roome and aboute the trunke and amonge the shooes and at the beds head; it came nearer the bed and Hanah was affraid and called father, but he heard not, wch made her more affraide; then cloathes were pulled of their bed by something, two or three times; they held and something pulled, wch frighted them so that Hanah Goodyeare called her father so loude as was thought might be heard to the meetinghouse, but the noise was heard to Mr. Samuell Eatons by them that watched wth her; so after a while Mr. Goodyeare came and found them in a great fright; they lighted a candell and he went to Eliza: Godmans chamber and asked her why she disturbed the family; she said no, she was scared also and thought the house had bine on fire, yet the next day she said in the family that she knew nothing till Mr. Goodyeare came up, wch she said is true she heard the noise but knew not the cause till Mr. Goodyeare came; and being asked why she went downe staires after she was gon up to bed, she said to light a candell to looke for two grapes she had lost in the flore and feared the mice would play wth them in the night and disturbe ye family, wch reason in the Courts apprehension renders her more suspitious.

Allen Ball informed the Court. Another time she came into his yard; his wife asked what she came for; she said to see her calfe; now they had a sucking calfe, wch they tyed in the lott to a great post that lay on ye ground, and the calfe ran away wth that post as if it had bine a fether and ran amonge Indian corne and pulled up two hills and stood still; after he tyed the calfe to a long heauy raile, as much as he could well lift, and one time she came into ye yard and looked on ye calfe and it set a running and drew the raile after it till it came to a fence and gaue a great cry in a lowing way and stood still; and in ye winter the calfe dyed, doe what he could, yet eate its meale well enough.

Some other passages were spoken of aboute Mris. Yale, that one time there being some words betwixt them, wth wch Eliza: Godman was unsatisfyed, the night following Mris. Yales things were throwne aboute the house in a strange manner; and one time being at Goodman Thorpes, aboute weauing some cloth, in wch something discontented her, and that night they had a great noise in the house, wch much affrighted them, but they know not what it was.

These things being declared the Court told Elizabeth Godman that they haue considered them, wth her former miscarriages, and see cause to order that she be comitted to prison, ther to abide the Courts pleasure, but because the matter is of weight, and the crime whereof she is suspected capitall, therefore she is to answer it at the Court of Magistrates in October next."

In October, 1655, Elizabeth "was again called before the court and told that upon grounds formerly declared wch stand upon record, she by her owne confession remains under suspition for witchcraft, and one more is now added, and that is, that one time this last summer, comeing to Mr. Hookes to beg some beare, was at first denyed, but after, she was offered some by his daughter which stood ready drawne, wch she had, yet went away in a muttering discontented manner, and after this, that night, though the beare was good and fresh, yet the next morning was hott, soure and ill tasted, yea so hott as the barrell was warme wthout side, and when they opened the bung it steemed forth; they brewed againe and it was so also, and so continewed foure or fiue times, one after another.

"She brought diuers psons to the court that they might say something to cleere her, and much time was spent in hearing ym, but to little purpose, the grounds of suspition remaining full as strong as before and she found full of lying, wherfore the court declared vnto her that though the euidenc is not sufficient as yet to take away her life, yet the suspitions are cleere and many, wch she cannot by all the meanes she hath vsed, free herselfe from, therfore she must forbeare from goeing from house to house to give offenc, and cary it orderly in the family where she is, wch if she doe not, she will cause the court to comitt her to prison againe, & that she doe now presently vpon her freedom giue securitie for her good behauiour; and she did now before the court ingage fifty pound of her estate that is in Mr. Goodyeers hand, for her good behauior, wch is further to be cleered next court, when Mr. Goodyeare is at home."

"She was suffered to dwell in the family of Thomas Johnson, where she continued till her death, October 9th, 1660." (*New Haven Town Records*, Vol. ii, pp. 174,179.)

NATHANIEL AND REBECCA GREENSMITH

Nathaniel Greensmith lived in Hartford, south of the little river, in 1661-62, on a lot of about twenty acres, with a house and barn. He also had other holdings "neer Podunk," and "on ye highway leading to Farmington."

He was thrifty by divergent and economical methods, since he is credited in the records of the time with stealing a bushel and a half of wheat, of stealing a hoe, and of lying to the court, and of battery.

In one way or another he accumulated quite a property for those days, since the inventory of it filed in the Hartford Probate Office, January 25, 1662, after his execution, carried an appraisal of £137. l4s. 1*d.*—including "2 bibles," "a sword," "a resthead," and a "drachm cup"—all indicating that Nathaniel judiciously mingled his theology and patriotism, his recreation and refreshment, with his everyday practical affairs and opportunities.

But he made one adventure that was most unprofitable. In an evil hour he took to wife Rebecca, relict of Abraham Elson, and also relict of Jarvis Mudge, and of whom so good a man as the Rev. John Whiting, minister of the First Church in Hartford—afterward first pastor of the Second Church—said that she was "a lewd, ignorant and considerably aged woman."

This triple combination of personal qualities soon elicited the criticism and animosity of the community, and Nathaniel and Rebecca fell under the most fatal of all suspicions of that day, that of being possessed by the evil one.

Gossip and rumor about these unpopular neighbors culminated in a formal complaint, and December 30, 1662, at a court held at Hartford, both the Greensmiths were separately indicted in the same formal charge.

"Nathaniel Greensmith thou art here indicted by the name of Nathaniel Greensmith for not having the fear of God before thine eyes, thou hast entertained familiarity with Satan, the grand enemy of God and mankind—and by his help hast acted things in a preternatural way beyond human abilities in a natural course for which according to the law of God and the established law of this commonwealth thou deservest to die."

While Rebecca was in prison under suspicion, she was interviewed by two ministers, Revs. Haynes and Whiting, as to the charges of Ann Cole—a next door neighbor—which were written down by them, all of which, and more, she confessed to be true before the court.

(Note. Increase Mather regarded this confession as convictive a proof of real witchcraft as most single cases he had known.)

THE MINISTERS' ACCOUNT—*Promise to Satan – A merry Christmas meeting – Stone's lecture – Haynes' plea – The dear Devil – The corvine guest – Sexual delusions*

"She forthwith and freely confessed those things to be true, that she (and other persons named in the discourse) had familiarity with the devil. Being asked whether she had made an express covenant with him, she answered she had not, only as she promised to go with him when he called (which she had accordingly done several times). But that the devil told her that at Christmas they would have a merry meeting, and then the covenant should be drawn and subscribed. Thereupon the fore-mentioned Mr. Stone (being then in court) with much weight and earnestness laid forth the exceeding heinousness and hazard of that dreadful sin; and therewith solemnly took notice (upon the occasion given) of the devil's loving Christmas.

"A person at the same time present being desired the next day more particularly to enquire of her about her guilt, it was accordingly done, to whom she acknowledged that though when Mr. Haynes began to read she could have torn him in pieces, and was so much resolved as might be to deny her guilt (as she had done before) yet after he had read awhile, she was as if her flesh had been pulled from her bones, (such was her expression,) and so could not deny any longer. She also declared that the devil first appeared to her in the form of a deer or fawn, skipping about her, wherewith she was not much affrighted but by degrees he contrived talk with her; and that their meetings were frequently at such a place, (near her own house;) that some of the company came in one shape and some in another, and one in particular in the shape of a crow came flying to them. Amongst other things she owned that the devil had frequent use of her body."

Had Rebecca been content with purging her own conscience, she alone would have met the fate she had invoked, and probably deserved; but out of "love to her husband's soul" she made an accusation against him, which of itself secured his conviction of the same offense, with the same dire penalty.

THE ACCUSATION—*Nathaniel's plea – "Travaile and labour" – "A red creature"--- Prenuptial doubts – The weighty logs – Wifely tenderness and anxiety – Under the greenwood tree – A cat call – Terpsichore and Bacchus*

"Rebecca Greenswith testifieth in Court Janry 8. 62.

"1. That my husband on Friday night last when I came to prison told me that now thou hast confest against thyself let me alone and say nothing of me and I wilbe good unto thy children.

"I doe now testifie that formerly when my husband hathe told me of his great travaile and labour I wondered at it how he did it this he did before I was married and when I was married I asked him how he did it and he answered me he had help yt I knew not of.

"3. About three years agoe as I think it; my husband and I were in ye wood several miles from home and were looking for a sow yt we lost and I saw a creature a red creature following my husband and when I came to him I asked him what it was that was with him and he told me it was a fox.

"4. Another time when he and I drove or hogs into ye woods beyond ye pound yt was to keep yong cattle severall miles of I went before ye hogs to call them and looking back I saw two creatures like dogs one a little blacker then ye other, they came after my husband pretty close to him and one did seem to me to touch him I asked him wt they were he told me he thought foxes I was stil afraid when I saw anything because I heard soe much of him before I married him.

"5. I have seen logs that my husband hath brought home in his cart that I wondered at it that he could get them into ye cart being a man of little body and weake to my apprhension and ye logs were such that I thought two men such as he could not have done it.

"I speak all this out of love to my husbands soule and it is much against my will that I am now necessitate to speake agaynst my husband, I desire that ye Lord would open his heart to owne and speak ye trueth.

"I also testify that I being in ye wood at a meeting there was wth me Goody Seager Goodwife Sanford & Goodwife Ayres; and at another time there was a meeting under a tree in ye green by or house & there was there James Walkely, Peter Grants wife Goodwife Aires & Henry Palmers wife of Wethersfield, & Goody Seager, & there we danced, & had a bottle of sack: it was in ye night & something like a catt cald me out to ye meeting & I was in Mr. Varlets orcherd wth Mrs. Judeth Varlett & shee tould me that shee was much troubled wth ye Marshall Jonath: Gilbert & cried, & she sayd if it lay in her power she would doe him a mischief, or what hurt shee could."

The Greensmiths were convicted and sentenced to suffer death. In January, 1662, they were hung on "Gallows Hill," on the bluff a little north of where Trinity College now stands—"a logical location" one most learned in the traditions and history of Hartford calls it—as it afforded an excellent view of the execution to a large crowd on the meadows to the west, a hanging being then a popular spectacle and entertainment.

CHAPTER IX

"They shall no more be considered guilty than this woman, whom I now pronounce to be innocent, and command that she be set at liberty." LORD CHIEF JUSTICE MANSFIELD.

ELIZABETH (CLAUSON) CLAWSON

THE INDICTMENT

"Elizabeth Clawson wife of Stephen Clawson of Standford in the country of Fayrefeild in the Colony of Connecticutt thou art here indicted by the name of Elizabeth Clawson that not haueing the fear of God before thine eyes thou hast had familiarity with Satan the grand enemie of God & man & that by his instigation & help thou hast in a pretematurall way afflicted & done harm to the bodyes & estates of sundry of his Maties subjects or to some of them contrary to the peace of or Soueraigne Lord the King & Queen their crowne & dignity & that on the 25t of Aprill in the 4th yeare of theire Maties reigne & at sundry other times for which by the law of God & the law of the Colony thou deseruest to dye."

THE TESTIMONIES

JOSEPH GARNEY—*The maid in fits—Joseph's subterfuge—""The black catt" — "The white dogg" —Witches three*

"Joseph Garney saith yt being at Danil Wescots uppon occation sine he went to Hartford while he was gone from home Nathanill Wiat being with me his maid being at work in the yard in her right mind soon after fell into a fit. I took her up and caried her in & laid her upon the bed it was intimated by sum that she desembled. Nathanel Wiat said with leaue he would make triall of that leaue was granted and as soon as she was laid upon ye bed then Wiat asked me for a sharp knife wch I presently took into my hand then she imediately came to herself and then went out of ye room into ye other room & so out into ye hen house then I hard her presently shreek out I ran presently to her and asked her what is ye matter, she was in such pain she could not Hue & presently fell into a fit stiff. We carried her in and laid her upon ye bed and then I got my kniffe ready and fitting under pretence of doing sum great matter then presently she came to herselfe & said to me Joseph what are you about to doe I said I would cutt her & seemed to threten great matters, then she laid her down upon the bed & said she would confess to us how it was with her and then said I am possessed with ye deuill and he apeared to me in ye hen house in ye shape of a black catt & was ernist with her to be a witch & if she would not he would tear her in pieces, then she again shreekt out now saith shee I see him & lookt wistly & said there he is just at this time to my apearance there seemed to dart in at ye west window a sudden light across ye room wch did startle and amase me at yt present, then she tould me yt she see ye deuill in ye shape of a white dogg, she tould me that ye deuill apeared in ye shape of these three women namly goody Clawson, goody Miller, & ye woman at Compo. [Disborough] I asked her how she knew yt it was ye deuill that appeared in ye shape of these three women she answered he tould me so. I asked her if she knew that these three women were witches or no she said she could not tell they might be honest women for ought she knew or they might be witches."

Sarah Kecham—*Cateron's seizures – Riding and singing – English and French – The naked sword*

The testimony of Sarah Kecham. "She saith yt being at Danel Wescots house Thomas Asten being there Cateron Branch being there in a fit as they said I asked then how she was they sayth she hath had noe fits she had bine a riding then I asked her to ride and then she got to riding. I asked her if her hors had any name & she called out & said Jack; I then asked her to sing & then she sunge; I asked her yt if she had sung wt Inglish she could then sing French and then she sung that wch they called French. Thomas Astin said he knew that she was bewitched I tould him I did not beleue it, for I said I did not beleue there was any witch in the town, he said he knew she was for said he I haue hard say that if a person were bewitched take a naked sword and hould ouer them & they will laugh themselues to death & with yt he took a sword and held ouer her and she laughed extremely. Then I spoke sumthing whereby I gaue them to understand that she did so becase she knew of ye sword, whereupon Danil made a sine to Thomas Austen to hould ye sword again yt she might not know of it, wch he did & then she did not laugh at all nor chang her countenance. Further in discourse I hard Daniel Wescot say yt when he pleased he could take her out of her fits. John Bates junr being present at ye same time witnesseth to all ye aboue written.

"Ye testers are redy to giue oath to ye aboue written testimony when called therunto. "Staford ye 7th Septembr 1692."

ABIGAIL CROSS AND NATHANIEL CROSS—*The "garles desembling" – Daniel Wescot's wager – The trick that nobody else could do*

(Kateran Branch, the accuser of the Fairfield women, was a young servant in Daniel Wescot's household.)

"The testimony of Abigail Cross as followith that upon sum discourse with Danil Wescot about his garles desembling sd Daniel sd that he would venture both his cows against a calfe yt she should doe a trick tomorrow morning that no body else could doe. sd Abigail sd to morrow morning, can you make her do it when you will; & he said yess when I will I can make her do it.

"Nathaneel Cross being present at ye same time testifieth ye same with his wife.

"The above testers say they are redy to giue oath to ye aboue written testimony when called to it."

SARAH BATES—*An effective remedy for fits – Burnt feathers – Blood letting – The result*

"The testimony of Mrs. Sarah Bates she saith yt when first ye garl was taken with strang fits she was sent for to Danil Wescots house & she found ye garle lieing upon ye bed. She then did apprehend yt the garls illness might be from sum naturall cause; she therefore aduised them to burn feathers under her nose & other menes yt had dun good in fainting fits and then she seemed to be better with it; and so she left her that night in hops to here she wold be better ye next morning; but in ye morning Danil Wescot came for her againe and when she came she found ye garl in bed seemingly senceless & spechless; her eyes half shet but her pulse seemed to beat after ye ordinary maner her mistres desired she might be let blud on ye foot in hops it might do her good. Then I said I thought it could not be dun in ye capassity she was in but she desired a triall to be made and when euerything was redy & we were agoing to let her blud ye garl cried; the reson was asked her why she cried; her answer was she would not be bluded; we asked her why; she said again because it would hurt her it was said ye hurt would be but small like a prick of a pin then she put her foot ouer ye bed and was redy to help about it; this cariag of her seemed to me strang who before seemed to ly like a dead creature; after she was bluded and had laid a short time she clapt her hand upon ye couerlid & cried out; and on of ye garls yt stood by said mother she cried out; and her mistres was so afected with it yt she cried and said she is bewitched. Upon this ye garl turned her head from ye folk as if she wold hide it in ye pillar & laughed." The above written Sarah Bates appeared before me in Stamford this 13th Septembr 1692 & made oath to the above written testimony. Before me Jonat, Bell Comissr."

Daniel Wescot—*Exchanging yarn* – *"A quarrill"* – *The child's nightmare*

"The testimony of Daniel Wescote saith that some years since my wife & Goodwife Clauson agreed to change their spinning, & instead of half a pound Goodwife Clawson sent three quarters of a pound I haueing waide it, carried it to her house & cnvinced her of it yt it was so, & thence forward she till now took occation upon any frivolous matter to be angry & pick a quarrill with booth myself & wife, & some short time after this earning ye flex, my eldest daughter Johannah was taken suddenly in ye night shrecking& crying out, There is a thing will catch me, uppon which I got up & lit a candle, & tould her there was nothing, she answerd, yees there was, there tis, pointing with her finger sometimes to one place & sometimes to another, & then sd tis run under the pillow. I askd her wr it was, she sd a sow, & in a like manner continued disturbd a nights abought ye space of three weeks, insomuch yt we ware forcd to carry her abroad sometimes into my yard or lot, but for ye most part to my next neighbours house, to undress her & get her to sleep, & continually wn she was disturbd shed cry out theres my thing come for me, whereuppon some neighbours advisd to a removal of her, &

having removd her to Fairfeild it left her, & since yt hath not been disturbd in like manner."

"The aboue testimony of Daniell Wesocott now read to the wife of sayd Daniell Shee testifys to the whole verbatum & hath now giuen oath to the same before us in Standford, Septembr 12th 1692.

"JONATN SELLECK Comissr

"JONOTHAN BELL Commissionr.

"Sworn in Court Septr 15 1692

"As attests John Allyn Secry."

ABIGAIL WESCOT—*Throwing stones—Railing—Twitting of "fine cloths"*

"Abigal Wescot further saith that as she was going along the street Goody Clauson came out to her and they had some words together and Goody Clauson took up stone and threw at her; and at another time as she went along the street before said Clausons dore Goody Clauson caled to me and asked me what I did in my chamber last Sabbath day night, and I doe affirme that I was not their that night; and at another time as I was in her sone Stephens house being neer her one house shee followed me in and contended with me becase I did not com into her house caling of me proud slut what ear you proud on your fine cloths and you look to be mistres but you never shal by me and seuerall other prouoking speeches at that time and at another time as I was by her house she contended and quareled with me; and we had many words together and shee twited me of my fine cloths and of my mufe and also contended with me several other times.

"Taken upon oath before us Standford Septemr 12th "JONATN SELLECK Comissionr "JONOTHAN BELL Comissr."

ABRAHAM FINCH—*The strange light—"Two pry eies"—Cause of the "pricking"*

"Abraham Finch jun aged about 26 years.

"The deponant saith that hee being a waching at with ye French girle at Daniell Wescoat house in the night I being laid on the bed the girle fell into a fite and fell crose my feet and then I looking up I sawe a light abut the bignes of my too hands glance along the sommer of the house to the harth ward, and afterwards I sawe it noe mor; and when Dauid Selleck brought a light into the room a littell space after the French garle cam to hirselfe againe. Wee ascked hir whie shee skreemed out when shee fell into her fit. Shee answered goodie Clawson cam in with two firy eies.

"Furdermore the deponant saith that Dauid Selleck was that same night with him and being laid downe on the bed me nie the garle and I laye by the bed sid on the chest and Dauid Selleck starte up suddenly and I asked wt was ye matter with him and hee answered shee pricked mee and the French garle answered noe shee did not it was goodie Crump and then shee put her hand ouer the bed sid and said give mee that thing that you pricked Mr. Selleck with and I cached hold of her hand and found a pin in it and I took it away from her. The deponant saith that when the garl put her hand ouer the bed it was open and he looked very well in her hand and cold see nothing and before shee puled in her hand again shee had goten yt pin yt hee took from her.

"This aboue written testor is redy when called to giue oath to the aboue written testimony."

EBENEZER BISHOP—*Kateran calls for somersaults – Fits and spots*

"Ebenezer Bishop aged about 26 years saith on night being at Danill Wescots house Catern Branch being in on of her fits I sate doen by ye bed side next to her she then calling ernestly upon goody Clason goody Clason seueral times now goody Clason turn heels ouer head after this she had a violent fit and calling again said now they are agoing to kill me & crieing out very loud that they pincht her on ye neck and calling out yt they pincht her again I setting by her I took ye light and look upon her neck & I see a spot look red seeming to me as big as a pece of eight afterwards it turned blue & blacker then any other part of her skin and after ye second time of her calling I took ye light & looked again and she pointed with her hand lower upon her shoulder and I se another place upon her shoulder look red & blue as I saw upon the other place before and then after yt she had another fit.

"Stamford 29th August 1692 this aboue written testor is redy when called to giue oath to ye aboue written testimony.

"Hannah Knapp testifieth the same to the above written and further adeth that shee saw scraches upon her; and is redy to give oth to it if called to it.

"Both the above sworn in Court Septr 15 1692. Attests John Allyn, Secry."

SAMUEL HOLLY – *Singular physiological transformations*

"The testimony of Samuel Holly senour aged aboute fifty years saith that hee being at ye house of Danell Wescot in ye euning I did see his maid Cattern Branch in her fit that shee did swell in her brests (as shee lay on her bed) and they rise as lik bladers and suddenly pased in to her bely, and in a short time returned to her brest and in a short time her breasts fell and a great ratling in her throat as if shee would haue been choked; All this I judge beyond nature.

"Danil Wescot testifieth to ye same aboue written and further addith yt when she was in those fits ratling in her throat she would put out her tong to a great extent I consieue beyond nature & I put her tong into her mouth again & then I looked in her mouth & could se no tong but as if it were a lump of flesh down her throat and this ofen times.

"The testors, as concerned are ready to giue oath to the above written testimony if called thereunto.

"Staford 29 April 1692

"Sworn in Court Septr 15 1692.

"Attests JOHN ALLYN, Seer."

"The testimony of Daniell Westcot aged about forty nine years saith that som time this spring since his maid Catton Branch had fits and with many other strange actions in her, I see her as shee lay on the bed at her length in her fit, and at once sprang up to the chamber flore withouts the helpe of her hands or feete; thats neere six feet and I judge it beyond nator for any person so to doe.

"Sworn in Court Sept 15 1692.

"Attests JOHN ALLYN Secry."

Inquiry and search – Visions of the young accuser – The talking cat – The spread table – The strange woman – "Silk hood and blew apron" – "2 firebrands in her forehead" – "A turn at heels ouer head"

"Stamford May ye 27th, 1692.

"Uppon ye information & sorrowfull complainte of Sergeant Daniel Wescot in regard of his maide servant Katherine Branch whome he suspects to be afflicted of witchcraft, under wch sore affliction she hath now labourd upwards of five weeks, & in that lamentable state yeat remains. In order to inquiry & search into (the) matter were then psent Major Nathan Golde, Capt. John Burr, Capt. Jonothan Selleck, Lieutenant Jonothan Bell.

"The manner of her being taken & handled.

"Being in ye feilds gathering of herbs, she was seizd with a pinching & pricking at her breast; she being come home fell a crying, was askd ye reason, gave no answer but wept & immediately fell down on ye flooer wth her hands claspt, & with like actions continued wth some respite at times ye space of two days, then sd she saw a cat, was asked what ye cat sd she answerd ye cat askd her to [go] with her, with a promise of fine things & yt if she should goe where there ware fine folks; & still was followed wth like fits, seeming to be much tormented, being askd again what she saw sd cats, & yt they toulde her they woulde kill her, & wth this menaceing disquieted her severall dayes; after yt she saw in ye roome where she lay a table spread wth variety of meats, & they askd her to eat & at ye table she saw tenn eating, this she positively affirmd when in her right minde, after this was exceeding much tormentted, her master askd her what was ye matter, because she as she sd in her fit run to sundry places to abscoude herselfe, she toulde him twas because she saw a cat coming to her wth a rat, to fling in her face, after yt she sd they toulde her they woulde kill her because she tould of it. These sort of actions continued about 13 days, & then was extremely afflicted with fits in ye night, to ye number of about 40ty crying out a witch, a witch, her master runing to her askd her what was ye matter she sd she felt a hand. Ye next week she saw as she sd a woman stand in ye house having on a silk hood & a blew apron, after that in ye evening being well composd going out of dooers run in again & caught her master abought ye middle, he askd her ye reason, she sd yt she meet an olde woman at ye dooer, with 2 firebrands in her forehead, he askd her what kinde of clooths she had on, answered she had two homespun coats, one tuct up rounde her ye other down. The next day she namd a person calling her goody Clauson, & sd there she is sitting on a reel, & again sd she saw her sit on ye pommel of a chair, saying Ime sure you are a witch, elce you coulde not sit so & sd she saw this person before namd at times for a week together. One time she sd she saw her and describd her whole attire, her [master]? went immediately & saw ye woman namd exactly atird as she was describd of ye person afflicted. Again she sd in her fits Goody Clauson lets haue a turn at heels ouer head, withall saying shall you goe first, or shall I. Weel sd she if I do first you shall after, & wth yt she turnd ouer two or three times heels ouer head, & so lay down, saying come if you will not Ile beat your head & ye wall together & haueing ended these words she goot up looking aboute ye house, & sd look shes gone, & so fell into a fit."

LIDIA PENOIR – "*A lying gairl*"

"The testimony of Lidia Penoir. Shee saith that shee heard her ant Abigal Wescot say that her seruant gairl Catern Branch was such a lying gairl that not any boddy could belieue one word what shee said and saith that shee heard her ant Abigail Wescot say that shee did not belieue that Mearcy nor goody Miller nor Hannah nor any of these women whome shee had apeacht was any more witches then shee was and that her husband would belieue Catern before he would belieue Mr. Bishop or Leiftenat Bell or herself.

"The testor is ready to giue oath to sd testimony. Standford, Augt 24th 1692."

ELEZER SLAWSON – "*A woman for pease*" – *A good word*

"The testimony of Elezer Slawson aged 51 year.

"He saith yt he liued neare neighbour, to goodwife Clawson many years & did allways observe her to be a woman for pease and to counsell for pease & when she hath had prouacations from her neighbours would answer & say we must liue in pease for we are naibours & would neuer to my obseruation giue threatning words nor did I look at her as one giuen to malice; & further saith not

"ELEAZAR SLASON. "CLEMENT BUXSTUM.

"The above written subscribers declared the aboue written & signed it with their own hands before me

"JONOTHAN BELL Comissionr."

In closing the citations of testimony in the Clawson case, other performances of Catherine Branch, the maid servant of Daniel and Abigail Wescot, are given to emphasize the absurdities which found credence in the community and brought several women to the bar of justice, to answer to the charge of a capital offense.

An epileptic fit – Muscular contortions – "Talkeing to the appearances" – "Hell fyre to all eternity" – A creature "with a great head & wings & noe boddy & all black" – Songs and tunes – Secular and scriptural recitations – " The lock of hayer"

"June 28th 1692.

"Sergt Daniell Wescott brought his Mayd Katheren Branch to my house to be examined, which was dune as is within mentioned, & the sd Katheren Branch being dismised was gott about 40 or 50 rodd from my house, my Indian girl runeing back sayinge sd Kate was falen downe & looked black in the face soe my sonn John Selleck & cousen Dauid Selleck went out & fecht her in, shee being in a stife fitt – & comeing out of that fitt fell a schrickeing, crying out you kill me, Goody Clawson you kill me, two or three times shee spoke it & her head was bent downe backwards allmost to her back; & sometimes her arme would be twisted round the sd Kate cryeing out you break my arme & with many such fitts following, that two men could hardly prevent by all their strenth the breaking of her neck & arme, as was thought by all the standers by; & in this maner sd Kate continued all the night, & neuer came to her sences but had som litell respitt betweene those teribile fitts & then sd Kate would be talkeing to the appearances & would answer them & ask questions of them to manny to be here inserted or remembered. They askt her to be as they were & then shee should be well & we herd sd Kate saye I will not yeald to you for you are wiches & yor portion is hell fyre to all eternity & many such like expressions shee had; telling them that Mr. Bishop had often tould her that shee must not yield to them, & that that daye Norwalk minister tould her the same therefore she sayd I hope God will keep me from yielding to you; sd Kate sayd Goody Clawson why doe you torment me soe; I neuer did you any harme neather in word nor acction; sayeing why are you all come now to afflict me. Katherine tould their names, saying Goody Clawson, Mercy Disbrow, Goody Miller, & a woman & a gail, five of you. Then she sd Kate spoke to the gail whom she caled Sarah, & sayd is Sarah Staples your right name; I am aferd you tell me a lye; tell me your rite name; & soe uged it much; & then stoped & sayd, tell; yeas I must tell my master & Capt. Selleck if they aske me but Ile tell noe body els. Soe at last sd Kate sayd, Hanah Haruy once or twice out is that your name why then did you tell me a lye before; Well then sayd Kate what is the womans name that comes with you; & soe stoped & then sayd tell yeas I must tell my master & Capt. Selleok if he askes me, but Ile tell noeboddy els, & sayd you will not tell me then I will ask Goody Crumpe;& she sd Gody Crump what is the woemans name yt comes with Hanah Haruy; & so urged severall times, a then sd Marry Mary what, & then Mary Haruy; well sayd Kate is Mary Haruy ye mother of Hanah Haruy; & then sayd now I know it seeming to reioyce, & saying Hanah why did you not tell me before, sayeing their was more catts come at first & I shall know all your names; & Kate sayd what creature is that with a great head & wings & noe boddy & all black, sayeing Hanah is that your father; I believe it is for you are a wich; & sd Kate sayd Hanah what is yor fathers name; & have you noe grandfather & grandmother; how come you to be a witch & then stoped, & sd again a grandmother what is her name & then stoped, & sd Goody Staples what is her maiden name & then again fell into terrible fits which much affrighted the standers by, which were many pesons to behould &

here what was sd & dune by Kate. Shee fell into a fitt singeing songes & then tunes as Kate sd giges for them to daunce by each takeing their turns; then sd Kate rehersed a great many verses, which are in some primers, & allsoe ye dialoge between Christ ye yoong man & the dieull, the Lords prayer, all the comand-ments & catechism, the creede & severall such good things, & then sayd, Hanah I will say noe more; let me here you, & sayd why doe I say these things; you doe not loue them & a great deale more she sayd which I cannot well remember but what is aboue & on ye other syde was herd and seene by myselfe & others as I've attest to it.

"Jonahn Selleck Commissioner."

"To add one thing more to my relation as is within of what I saw & herd, is that som persons atempted to cutt of a lock of the sd Kates hayer, when shee was in her fitts but could not doe it, for allthough she knew not what was sayd & dune by them, & let them come neuer soe priuately behynd her to doe it yeat shee would at once turne about and preuent it; At last Dauid Waterbery tooks her in his armes to hould her by force; that a lock of hayer might be cutt; but though at other times a weake & light gail yeat shee was then soe stronge & soe extreame heauy that he could not deale with her, not her hayer could not be cutt; & Kate cryeing out biterly, as if shee had bin beaten all ye time. When sd Kate come to herself, was askt if she was wileing her hayer should be cutt; shee answered yeas—we might cutt all of it we would."

Elizabeth Clawson was found not guilty.

HUGH (CROSIA, CROSHER) CROHSAW

A court of Assistants holden at Hartford, May 8th, 1693.

Present.

Robert Treat, Esq. Governor

William Joanes, Esq. Dept. Govr.

Samuel Willis, Esq.

William Pitkin, Esq. } Assistants

Col. John Allyn

Nath. Stanly, Esq.

Caleb Stanly, Esq.

Moses Mansfield, Esq.

Gent. of the Jury are:

Joseph Bull, Nathaneal Loomis, Joseph Wadsworth, Nathanael Bowman, Jonathan Ashley, Stephen Chester, Daniel Heyden, Samuell Newell, Abraham Phelps, Joseph North, John Stoughton, Thomas Ward.

And the names of the Grand Jury are: Bartholomew Barnard, Joseph Mygatt, William Williams, John Marsh, John Pantry, Joseph Langton, William Gibbons, Stephen Kelsey, Cornelious Gillett, Samuel Collins, James Steele, Jonathan Loomis.

THE INDICTMENT

"Hugh Crotia, Thou Standest here presented by the Name of Hugh Crotia of Stratford in the Colony of Connecticutt, in New England; for that not haveing the fear of God before thine Eyes, through the Instigation of the Devill, thou hast forsaken thy God, & covenanted with the Devill, and by his help hast in a preternaturall way afflicted the bodys of Sundry of his Majestie's good subjects, for which according to the Law of God, and the Law of this Colony, thou deservest to dye."

The arrest – Satan the accessory – An alibi – The confession – A contract to serve the devil

"Fayrfield this 15 Novembor 1692 acording as is Informed that hugh Crosia is complained of by a gerll at Stratford for aflicting her and hee being met on ye road going westward from fayrfeild hee being met by Joseph Stirg and danill bets of norwak and being brought back by them to athority in fayrfeild and on thare report to sd authority of sum confesion sd Croshaw mad of such things as rendar him undar suspecion of familiarity with satan sd Crosha being asked whethar he sayd he sent ye deuell to hold downe Eben Booths gerll ye gerll above intended hee answared hee did say so but hee was not thar himself hee answereth he lyed when he sayd he sent ye deuell as above.

"Sd hugh beeing asked whethar hee did not say hee had made a Contract with ye deuell five years senc with his heart and signed to ye deuells book and then seald it with his bloud which Contract was to serve ye deuell and the deuell to serve him he saith he did say so and sayd he ded so and wret his name and sealed ye Contract with his bloud and that he had ever since been practising Eivel against every man: hee also sayd ye deuell opned ye dore of eben booths hous made it fly open and ye gate fly open being asked how he could tell he sayd he deuell apeered to him like a boye and told him hee ded make them fly open and then ye boye went out of his sight.

"This examination taken and Confessed before authority in fairefeild before Us Testis the date above "Jon. Bur, Assist "Nathan Gold, Asist."

"The Grand Jury upon consideration of this Case re-turnd, Ignoramus....

"This Court do grant to the said Hugh Crotia A Gaol Delivery, he paying the Master of the Gaol his just fees and dues upon his release and also all the Charge laid out on him at Fairfield, & in bringing him to prison.

ELIZABETH GARLICK

In 1657, when Easthampton, Long Island, was within the jurisdiction of New York, becoming a few months later a part of Connecticut, two persons came over from Gardiner's Island and settled in the colony, Joshua Garlick and Elizabeth his wife—whilom servants of the famous engineer and colonist Lion Gardiner.

Stories of Elizabeth's practice of witchcraft and other black arts followed her, and despite her attendance at church she fell under suspicion, and was arrested, and held by the magistrates for trial after hearing various witnesses. Credulity offers no better illustrations than those which fell from the lips of some of the witnesses in this case.

Tuning a psalm – A black thing – A double tongued woman – A doleful noise – Burning the herbs – The sick child – Gardiner's ox – The dead ram – Burning "the sow's tale"

Goodwife Howell, during her illness which hastened Elizabeth's arrest, "tuned a psalm and screked out several times together very grievously," and cried "a witch! a witch! now are you come to torter me because I spoke two or three words against you," and also said, she saw a black thing at the beds featte, that Garlick was double-tongued, pinched her with pins, and stood by the bed ready to tear her in pieces. And William Russell, in a fit of insomnia or indigestion, before daybreak, "heard a very doleful noyse on ye backside of ye fire, like ye noyse of a great stone thrown down among a heap of stones."

Goody Birdsall "declared y't she was in the house of Goody Simons when Goody Bishop came into the house with ye dockweed and between Goody Davis and Goody Simons they burned the herbs. Farther, she said y't formerly dressing flax at Goody Davis's house, Goody D>avis saith y't she had dressed her children in clean linen at the island, and Goody Garlick came in and said, 'How pretty the child doth look,' and so soon as she had spoken Goody Garlick said, 'the child is not well, for it groaneth,' and Goody Davis said her heart did rise, and Goody Davis said, when she took the child from Goody Garlick, she said she saw death in the face of it, & her child sickened presently upon it, and lay five daies and 5 nights and never opened the eyes nor dried till it died. Also she saith as she dothe remember Goody Davis told her upon some difference between Mr. Gardiner or some of his family, Goodman Garlick gave out some threateningse speeches, & suddenly after Mr. Gardiner had an ox legge broke upon Ram Island. Moreover Goody Davis said that Goody Garlick was a naughtie woman."

Goody Edwards testified: "Y't as Goody Garlick owned, she sent to her daughter for a little best milk and she had some and presently after, her daughters milk went away as she thought and as she remembers the child sickened about y't time." Goody Hand deposed that "she had heard Goody Davis say that she hoped Goody Garlick would not come to Eastharapton, because, she said, Goody Garlick was naughty, and there had many sad things befallen y'm at the Island, as about ye child, and ye ox, as Goody Birdsall have declared, as also the negro child she said was taken away, as I understood by her words, in a strange manner, and also of a ram y't was dead, and this fell out quickly one after another, and also of a sow y't was fat and lustie and died. She said they did burn some of the sow's tale and presently Goody Garlick did come in.">

The settlers held a town meeting, and wisely questioning whether they had legal authority to hold a trial in a capital case, they ap pointed a committee to go "unto Keniticut to carry up Goodwife Garlick yt she may be delivered up unto the authoritie there for the trial of the cause of witchcraft which she is suspected for." The General Court of Connecticut took jurisdiction of the case, a trial of Goody Garlick was held, resulting in her acquittal, and she was sent back to Easthampton, to what end is not told in the records of the day.

CHAPTER X

"This case is one of the most painful in the entire Connecticut list, for she impresses one as the best woman; how the just and high minded old lady had excited hate or suspicion, we cannot know." *Connecticut as a Colony* (1: 212), MORGAN.

"Mr. Dauenport gaue in as followeth—That Mr. Ludlow sitting with him and his wife alone, and discoursing of the passages concerning Knapps wife, the Witch and her execution, said that she came downe from the ladder (as he understood it), and desired to speak with him alone, and told him who was the witch spoken of." *New Haven Colonial Record* (2: 78).

"Shortly after this, a poor simple minded woman living in Fairfield, by the name of Knap, was suspected of witchcraft. She was tried, condemned and sentenced to be hanged." SCHENCK'S *History of Fairfield* (1: 71).

"GOODWIFE KNAP"

This was one of the most notable of the witchcraft cases. It stands among the early instances of the infliction of the death penalty in Connecticut; the victim was presumably a woman of good repute, and not a common scold, an outcast, or a harridan; it is singularly illustrative of witchcraft's activities and their grasp on the lives of the best men and women, of the beliefs that ruled the community, and of the crude and revolting practices resorted to in the punishments of the condemned, and especially since in its later developments it involved in controversy and litigation two of the great characters in colonial history, Rev. John Davenport, one of the founders of New Haven, and Roger Ludlow, Deputy Governor of Massachusetts and Connecticut. [I] Goodwife Knapp of Fairfield was "suspicioned." That was enough to set the villagers agog with talk and gossip and scandal about the unfortunate woman, which poisoned the wells of sober thought and charitable purpose, and swiftly ripened into a formal accusation and indictment.

[I] Connecticut, through its Commission of Sculpture, in recognition of his services to the Colony, is to erect a memorial statue to Ludlow to occupy the western niche on the northern facade of the Capitol building at Hartford.

Pending her trial the prisoner was committed to the house of correction or common jail for the safe keeping of "refractory persons" and criminals.

What terrors of mind and spirit must have waited on this "simple minded" woman, in the cold, gloomy, and comfortless prison, probably built of rough logs, with a single barred window and massive iron studded door, a ghost haunted torture chamber, in charge of some harsh wardsmen.

Knapp was duly and truly tried, and sentenced to death by hanging, the usual mode of execution. *No witch was ever burned in New England.*

From the day sentence was pronounced until the hanging took place, out in Try's field beyond the Indian field, in view of the villagers, whose curiosity or thirst for horrors or whose duty led them there, this prisoner of delusion was made the object of rudest treatment, espionage, and of inhuman attempts to wring from her lips a confession of her own guilt or an accusation against some other person as a witch.

The very day of her condemnation, a self-constituted committee of women, with one man on it,—Mistress Thomas Sherwood, Goodwife Odell, Mistress Pell, and her two daughters, Goody Lockwood, and Goodwife Purdy,—visited the prison, and pressed her to name any other witch in town, and so receive such consolation from the minister as would be for her soul's welfare.

Mistress Pell seems to have been the chief spokeswoman, and each member of the committee served in some degree as an inquisitor, or exhorter, not to repentance, but to disclosures. Baited and badgered, warned and threatened, the hapless prisoner protested she was innocent, denied the charges made against her, told one of the committee to "take heed the devile have not you," and also said, "I must not render evil for evil.... I have sins enough allready, and I will not add this [accusing another] to my condemnation." And at last in agony of soul she made that pathetic appeal to one of her relentless tormentors, "neuer, neuer poore creature was tempted as I am tempted, pray, pray for me."

But even after death on the scaffold, the witch-hunters of the day did not refrain from their ghoulish work, but desecrated the remains of Goodwife Knapp at the grave side in their search for witch marks.

All the facts during the imprisonment, execution and burial are set forth in some of the testimonies herewith given, in a chapter of related history (the evidence at the trial not being disclosed in any present record), and all of them marked by a total unconsciousness of their sinister and revolting character.

No case in the history of the delusion in New England is more replete in incidents and apt illustrations, due to their fortunate preservation in the records of a lawsuit involving some of the prominent characters in that drama of religious insanity.

At a magistrate's court held at New Haven the 29th of May, 1654.

Present.

Theophilus Eaton Esqr, Gouernor.

Mr. Stephen Goodyeare, Dept, Gouernor.

Francis Newman

Mr. William Fowler

Mr. William Leete

} Magistrats

a suit was heard entitled—

Thomas Staplies of Fairfield, plant'.

Mr Rogger Ludlow late of Fairfield, defendt.

It was brought by an aggrieved husband to recover damages for defamation of the character of his wife. It centered in one of the dramatic incidents at Knapp's execution. In the last extremity, and in the presence of immediate death, the prisoner came down from the ladder, and asking to speak with Ludlow alone, told him that Goodwife Staplies was a witch.

Some time afterward Ludlow, at New Haven, told the Rev. John Davenport and his wife the story, in confidence, and under the promise of secrecy, but it spread abroad with inevitable accretions, and when it reached Fairfield Thomas Staplies went to law, to vindicate his wife's character in pounds, shillings, and pence. These are some of the statements and remarkable testimonies:

Attorney Banke's declaration – Ensigne Bryan's answer – Davenport's view of an oath, Hebrews vi,16 – His account and conscientious scruples – Mistress Davenport's forgetfulness – "A tract of lying" – "Indian gods" – Luce Pell and Hester Ward's visit to the prison – The "search" of Knapp – "Witches teates" – Feminine resemblances – Matronly opinions – Post-mortem evidence – Contradictions – Knapp's ordeal – "Fished wthall in private" – Her denials – Talk on the road to the "gallowes"

"John Bankes, atturny for Thomas Staplies, declared, that Mr. Ludlow had defamed Thomas Staplies wife, in reporting to Mr. Dauenport and Mris. Dauenport that she had laid herselfe vnder a new suspition of being a witch, that she had caused Knapps wife to be new searched after she was hanged, and when she saw the teates, said if they were the markes of a witch, then she was one, or she had such markes; secondly, Mr. Ludlow said Knapps wife told him that goodwife Staplies was a witch; thirdly, that Mr. Ludlow hath slandered goodwife Staplies in saying that she made a trade of lying, or went on in a tract of lying, &c.

"Ensigne Bryan, atturny for Mr. Ludlow, desired the charge might bee proued, wch accordingly the plant' did, and first an attestation vnder Master Dauenports hand, conteyning the testimony of Master and Mistris Dauenport, was presented and read; but the defendant desired what was testified and accepted for proofe might be vpon oath, vpon wch Mr. Dauenport gaue in as followeth, That he hoped the former attestation hee wrott and sent to the court, being compared wth Mr. Ludlowes letter, and Mr. Dauenports answer, would haue satisfyed concerning the truth of the pticulars wthout his oath, but seeing Mr. Ludlowes atturny will not be so satisfyed, and therefore the court requires his oath, and yt he lookes at an oath, in a case of necessitie, for confirmation of truth, to end strife among men, as an ordinance of God, according to Heb: 6,16, hee therevpon declares as followeth,

"That Mr. Ludlow, sitting wth him & his wife alone, and discoursing of the passages concerning Knapps wife the witch, and her execution, said that she came downe from the ladder, (as he vnderstood it,) and desired to speake wth him alone, and told him who was the witch spoken of; and so fair as he remembers, he or his wife asked him who it was; he said she named goodwife Stapleies; Mr. Dauenport replyed that hee beleeued it was vtterly vntrue and spoken out of malice, or to that purpose; Mr. Ludlow answered that he hoped better of her, but said she was a foolish woman, and then told them a further storey, how she tumbled the corpes of the witch vp & downe after her death, before sundrie women, and spake to this effect, if these be the markes of a witch I am one, or I haue such markes. Mr. Dauenport vtterly disliked the speech, not haueing heard anything from others in that pticular, either for her or against her, and supposing Mr. Ludlow spake it vpon such intelligenc as satisfyed him; and whereas Mr. Ludlow saith he required and they promised secrecy, he doth not remember that either he required or they pmised it, and he doth rather beleeue the contrary, both because he told them that some did ouerheare what the witch said to him, and either had or would spread it abroad, and because he is carefull not to make vnlawfull promises, and when he hath made a lawfull promise he is, through the help of Christ, carefull to keepe it.

"Mris. Dauenport saith, that Mr. Ludlow being at their house, and speakeing aboute the execution of Knapps wife, (he being free in his speech,) was telling seuerall passages of her, and to the best of her remembrance said that Knapps wife came downe from the ladder to speake wth him, and told him that goodwife Staplyes was a witch, and that Mr. Daueport replyed something on behalfe of goodwife Staplies, but the words she remembers not; and something Mr. Ludlow spake, as some did or might ouer-heare what she said to him, or words to that effect, and that she tumbled the dead body of Knapps wife vp & downe and spake words to this purpose, that if these be the markes of a witch she was one, or had such markes; and concerning any promise of secrecy she remembers not."

"Mr. Dauenport and Mris. Dauenport affirmed ypon oath, that the testimonies before written, as they properly belong to each, is the truth, according to their best knowledg & memory.

"Mr. Dauenport desired that in takeing his oath to be thus vnderstood, that as he takes his oath to giue satisfaction to the court and Mr. Ludlowes atturny, in the matters attested betwixt M' Ludlow & Thomas Staplies, so he lymits his oath onely to that pt and not to ye preface or conclusion, they being no pt of the attestation and so his oath not required in them.

"To the latter pt of the declaration, the plant' pduced ye proofe following,

"Goodwif Sherwood of Fairfeild affirmeth vpon oath, that vpon some debate betwixt Mr. Ludlow and goodwife Staplies, she heard M' Ludlow charge goodwif Staplies wth a tract of lying, and that in discourse she had heard him so charge her seuerall times.

"John Tompson of Fairfeild testifyeth vpon oath, that in discourse he hath heard Mr. Ludlow express himselfe more then once that goodwife Staplies went on in a tract of lying, and when goodwife

Staplyes hath desired Mr. Ludlow to convince her of telling one lye, he said she need not say so, for she went on in a tract of lying.

"Goodwife Gould of Fairefeild testifyeth vpon oath, that in a debate in ye church wth Mr. Ludlow, goodwife Staplyes desired him to show her wherein she had told one lye, but Mr. Ludlow said she need not mention ptculars, for she had gon on in a tract of lying.

"Ensigne Bryan was told, he sees how the plantife hath proued his charge, to wch he might now answer; wherevpon he presented seuerall testimonies in wrighting vpon oath, taken before Mr. Wells and Mr. Ludlow.

"May the thirteenth, 1654.

"Hester Ward, wife of Andrew Ward, being sworne deposeth, that aboute a day after that goodwife Knapp was condemned for a witch, she goeing to ye prison house where the said Knapp was kept, she, ye said Knapp, voluntarily, wthout any occasion giuen her, said that goodwife Staplyes told her, the said Knapp, that an Indian brought vnto her, the said Staplyes, two litle things brighter then the light of the day, and told the said goodwife Staplyes they were Indian gods, as the Indian called ym; and the Indian wthall told her, the said Staplyes, if she would keepe them, she would be so big rich, all one god, and that the said Staplyes told the said Knapp, she gaue them again to the said Indian, but she could not tell whether she did so or no.

"Luce Pell, the wife of Thomas Pell, being sworne deposeth as followeth, that aboute a day after goodwife Knapp was condemned for a witch, Mris. Jones earnestly intreated her to goe to ye said Knapp, who had sent for her, and then this deponent called the said Hester Ward, and they went together; then the said Knapp voluntarily, of her owne accord, spake as the said Hester Ward hath testifyed, word by word; and the said Mris. Pell further saith, that she being one of ye women that was required by the court to search the said Knapp before she was condemned, & then Mris. Jones presed her, the said Knapp, to confess whether ther were any other that were witches, because goodwife goodwife Basset, when she was condemned, said there was another witch in Fairefeild that held her head full high, and then the said goodwife Knapp stepped a litle aside, and told her, this deponent, goodwife Basset ment not her;

she asked her whom she ment, and she named goodwife Staplyes, and then vttered the same speeches as formerly conerning ye Indian gods, and that goodwife Staplyes her sister Martha told the said goodwife Knapp, that her sister Staplyes stood by her, by the fire in there house, and she called to her, sister, sister, and she would not answer, but she, the said Martha, strucke at her and then she went away, and ye next day she asked her sister, and she said she was not there; and Mris. Ward doth also testify wth Mris. Pell, that the said Knapp said the same to her; and the said Mris. Pell saith, that aboute two dayes after the search afforesaid, she went to ye said Knapp in prison house, and the said Knapp said to her, I told you a thing the other day, and goodman Staplies had bine wth her and threatened her, that she had told some thing of his wife that would bring his wiues name in question, and this deponent she told no body of it but her husband, & she was much moued at it.

"Elizabeth Brewster being sworne, deposeth and saith, that after goodwife Knap was executed, as soone as she was cut downe, she, the said Knapp, being caried to the graue side, goodwife Staplyes wth some other women went to search the said Knapp, concerning findeing out teats, and goodwife Staplyes handled her verey much, and called to goodwife Lockwood, and said, these were no witches teates, but such as she herselfe had, and other women might haue the same, wringing her hands and takeing ye Lords name in her mouth, and said, will you say these were witches teates, they were not, and called vpon goodwife Lockwood to come & see them; then this deponent desired goodwife Odell to come & see, for she had bine vpon her oath when she found the teates, and she, this depont, desired the said Odill to come and clere it to goodwife Staplies; goodwife Odill would not come; then the said Staplies still called vpon goodwife Lockwood to come, will you say these are witches teates, I, sayes the said Staplies, haue such myselfe, and so haue you if you search yorselfe; goodwife Lockwood replyed, if I had such, she would be hanged; would you, sayes Staplies, yes, saith Lockwood, and deserve it; and the said Staplies handeled the said teates very much, and pulled them wth her fingers, and then goodwife Odill came neere, and she, the said Staplies, still questioning, the said Odill told her no honest woman had such, and then all the women rebuking her and said they were witches teates, and the said Staplies yeilded it.

"Mary Brewster being sworn & deposed, saith as followeth, that she was present after the execution of ye said Knapp, and she being brought to the graue side, she saw goodwife Staplyes pull the teates that were found aboute goodwife Knapp, and was verey earnest to know whether those were witches teates wch were found aboute her, the said Knapp, wn the women searched her, and the said Staplyes pulled them as though she would haue pulled them of, and prsently she, ths depont, went away, as hauing no desire to looke vpon them.

"Susan Lockwood, wife of Robert Lockwood, being sworne & examined saith as foll, that she was at the execution of goodwife Knapp that was hanged for a witch, and after the said Knapp was cut downe and brought to the graue, goodwife Staplyes, wth other women, looked after the teates that the women spake of appointed by the magistrats, and the said goodwife Staplies was handling of her where the teates were, and the said Staplies stood vp and called three or foure times and bid me come looke of them, & asked her whether she would say they were teates, and she made this answer, no matter whether there were teates or no, she had teates and confessed she was a witch, that was sufficient; if these be teates, here are no more teates then I myselfe haue, or any other women, or you either if you would search yor body; this depont saith she said, I know not what you haue, but for herselfe, if any finde any such things aboute me, I deserved to be hanged as she was, and yet afterward she, the said Staplyes, stooped downe againe and handled her, ye said Knapp, verey much, about ye place where the teates were, and seuerall of ye women cryed her downe, and said they were teates, and then she, the said Staplyes, yeilded, & said verey like they might be teates.

"Thomas Sheruington & Christopher Combstocke & goodwife Baldwine were all together at the prison house where goodwife Knapp was, and ye said goodwife Baldwin asked her whether she, the said Knapp, knew of any other, and she said there were some, or one, that had receiued Indian gods that were very bright; the said Baldwin asked her how she could tell, if she were not a witch herselfe, and she said the party told her so, and her husband was witnes to it; and to this they were all sworne & doe depose.

"Rebecka Hull, wife of Cornelius Hull, being sworne & examined, deposeth & saith as followeth, that when goodwife Knapp was goeing to execution, Mr. Ludlow, and her father Mr. Jones, pressing the said Knapp to confess that she was a witch, vpon wch goodwife Staplies said, why should she, the said Knapp, confess that wch she was not, and after she, the said goodwife Staplyes, had said so, on that stood by, why should she say so, she the said Staplyes replyed, she made no doubt if she the said Knapp were one, she would confess it.

"Deborah Lockwood, of the age of 17 or thereaboute, sworne & examined, saith as followeth, that she being present when goodwife Knapp was goeing to execution, betweene Tryes & the mill, she heard goodwife Staplyes say to goodwife Gould, she was pswaded goodwife Knapp was no witch; goodwife Gould said, sister Staplyes, she is a witch, & hath confessed had had familiarity wth the Deuill. Staplies replyed, I was wth her yesterday, or last night, and she said no such thing as she heard.

"Aprill 26th, 1654.

"Bethia Brundish, of the age of sixteene or thereaboutes, maketh oath, as they were goeing to execution of goodwife Knapp, who was condemned for a witch by the court & jury at Fairfeild, there being present herselfe & Deborah Lockwood and Sarah Cable, she heard goodwife Staplyes say, that she thought the said goodwife Knapp was no witch, and goodwife Gould presently reproued her for it." "Witnes

"Andrew Warde,

"Jurat' die & anno prdicto,

"Coram me, Ro Ludlowe.

"The plant' replyed that he had seuerall other witnesses wch he thought would cleere the matters in question, if the court please to heare them, wch being granted, he first presented a testimony of goodwife Whitlocke of Fairfeild, vpon oath taken before Mr. Fowler at Millford, the 27th of May, 1654, wherein she saith, that concerning goodwife Staplyes speeches at the execution of goodwife Knapp, she being present & next to goody Staplyes when they were goeing to put the dead corpes of goodwife Knapp into the graue, seuerall women were looking for the markes of a witch vpon the dead body, and seuerall of the women said they could finde none, & this depont said, nor I; and she heard goodwife Staplyes say, nor I; then came one that had searched the said witch, & shewed them the markes that were vpon her, and said what are these; and then this depont heard goodwife Staplyes say she never saw such in all her life, and that she was pswaded that no honest woman had such things as those were; and the dead corps being then prsently put into the graue, goodwife Staplyes & myselfe came imediately away together vnto the towne, from the place of execution.

"Goodwife Barlow of Fairfeild before the court did now testify vpon oath, that when Knapps wife was hanged and ready to be buried, she desired to see the markes of a witch and spake to one of her neighbours to goe wth her, and they looked but found them not; then goodwife Staplyes came to them, and one or two more, goodwife Stapyleyes kneeled downe by them, and they all looked but found ym not, & said they saw nothing but what is comon to other women, but after they found them they all wondered, and goodwife Staplyes in pticular, and said they neuer saw such things in their life before, so they went away.

"The wife of John Tompson of Fairefeild testifyeth vpon oath, that goodwife Whitlock, goodwife Staplyes and herselfe, were at the graue and desired to see ye markes of the witch that was hanged, they looked but found them not at first, then the midwife came & shewed them, goodwife Staplyes said she neuer saw such, and she beleeved no honest woman had such.

"Goodwife Sherwood of Fairefeild testifyeth vpon oath, that that day Knapps wife was condemned for a witch, she was there to see her, all being gone forth but goodwife Odill and her selfe, then their came in Mris. Pell and her two daughters, Elizabeth & Mary, goody Lockwood and goodwife Purdy; Mris. Pell told Knapps wife she was sent to speake to her, to haue her confess that for wch she was condemned, and if she knew any other to be a witch to discover them, and told her, before she was condemned she might thinke it would be a meanes to take away her life, but now she must dye, and therefore she should discouer all, for though she and her family by the providence of God had brought in nothing against her, yet ther was many witnesses came in against her, and she was cast by the jury & godly magistrats hauing found her guilty, and that the last evidence cast the cause. So the next day she went in againe to see the witch wth other neighbours, there was Mr. Jones, Mris. Pell & her two daughters, Mris. Ward and goodwife Lockwood, where she heard Mris. Pell desire Knapps wife to lay open herselfe, and make way for the minister to doe her good; her daughter Elizabeth bid her doe as the witch at the other towne did, that is, discouer all she knew to be witches. Goodwife Knapp said she must not say anything wch is not true, she must not wrong any body, and what had bine said to her in private, before she went out of the world, when she was vpon the ladder, she would reveale to Mr. Ludlow or ye minister. Elizabeth Bruster said, if you keepe it a litle longer till you come to the ladder, the diuill will haue you quick, if you reveale it not till then. Good: Knapp replyed, take heed the devile haue not you, for she could not tell how soone she might be her companyon, and added, the truth is you would haue me say that goodwife Staplyes is a witch, but I haue sinns enough to answer for allready, and I hope I shall not add to my condemnation; I know nothing by goodwife Staplyes, and I hope she is an honest woman. Then goodwife Lockwood said, goodwife Knapp what ayle you; goodman Lyon, I pray speake, did you heare vs name goodwif Staplyes name since we came here; Lyon wished her to haue a care what she said and not breed difference betwixt neighbours after she was gone; Knapp replyed, goodman Lyon hold yor tongue, you know not what I know, I haue ground for what I say, I haue bine fished wthall in private more then you are aware of; I apprehend goodwife Staples hath done me some wrong in her testimony, but I must not render euill for euill. Then this depont spake to goody Knapp, wishing her to speake wth the jury, for she apprehended goodwife Staplyes witnessed nothing contrary to other witnesses, and she supposed they would informe her that the last evidence did not cast ye cause; she replyed that she had bine told so wthin this halfe houre, & desired Mr. Jones and herselfe to stay and the rest to depart, that she might speake wth vs in private, and desired me to declare to Mr. Jones what they said against goodwife Staplyes the day before, but she told her she heard not goodwife Staplyes named, but she knew nothing of that nature; she desired her to declare her minde fully to M' Jones, so she went away.

"Further this depont saith, that comeing into the house where the witch was kept, she found onely the wardsman and goodwife Baldwine, there goodwife Baldwin whispered her in the eare and said to her that goodwife Knapp told her that a woman in ye towne was a witch and would be hanged wthin a twelue moneth, and would confess herselfe a witch and cleere her that she was none, and that she asked her how she knew she was a witch, and she told her she had reeived Indian gods of an Indian, wch are shining things, wch shine lighter then the day. Then this depont asked goodwife Knapp if she had said so, and she denyed it; goodwife Baldwin affirmed she did, but Knapps wife againe denyed it and said she knowes no woman in the towne that is a witch, nor any woman that hath received Indian gods, but she said there was an Indian at a womans house and offerred her a coople of shining things, but she woman neuer told her she tooke them, but was afraide and ran away, and she knowes not that the woman euer tooke them. Goodwife desired this depont to goe out and speake wth the wardsmen; Thomas Shervington, who was one of them, said hee remembred not that Knapps wife said a woman in the towne was a witch and would be hanged, but spake something of shining things, but Kester, Mr. Pells man, being by said, but I remember; and as they were goeing to the graue, goodwife Staplyes said, it was long before she could beleeve this poore woman was a witch, or that their were any witches, till the word of God convinced her, wch saith, thou shalt not suffer a witch to liue.

"Thomas Lyon of Fairfeild testifyeth vpon oath, taken before Mr. Fowler, the 27th May, 1654, that he being set by authority to watch wth Knapps wife, there came in Mris. Pell, Mrs. Ward, goodwife Lockwood, and Mris. Pells two daughters; the fell into some discourse, that goodwife Knapp should say to them in private wch goodwife Knapp would not owne, but did seeme to be much troubled at them and said, the truth is you would haue me to say that goodwife Staplyes is a witch; I haue sinnes enough allready, I will not add this to my condemnation, I know no such thing by her, I hope she is an honest woman; then goodwife Lockwood caled to mee and asked whether they had named goodwife Staplyes, so I spake to goodwife Knapp to haue a care what she said, that she did not make differrence amongst her neighbours when she was gon, and I told her that I hoped they were her frends and desired her soules good, and not to accuse any out of envy, or to that effect; Knapps wife said, goodman Lyon hold yor tongue, you know not so much as I doe, you know not what hath bine said to me in private; and after they was gon, of her owne accord, betweene she & I, goody Knapp said she knew nothing against goodwife Staplyes of being a witch.

"Goodwife Gould of Fairfeild testifyeth vpon oath, that goodwife Sherwood & herselfe came in to see the witch, there was one before had bine speaking aboute some suspicious words of one in the towne, this depont wished her if she knew anything vpon good ground she would declare it, if not, that she would take heede that the deuill pswaded her not to sow malicious seed to doe hurt when she was dead, yet wished her to speake the truth if she knew anything by any pson; she said she knew nothing but vpon suspicion by the rumours she heares; this depont told her she was now to dye, and therefore she should deale truly; she burst forth ito weeping and desired me to pray for her, and said I knew not how she was tempted; neuer, neuer poore creature was tempted as I am tempted, pray, pray for me. Further this depont saith, as they were goeing to ye graue, Mr. Buckly, goodwife Sherwood, goodwife Staplye and myselfe, goodwife Staplyes was next me, she said it was a good while before she could beleeue this woman was a witch, and that she could not beleue a good while that there were any witches, till she went to ye word of God, and then she was convinced, and as she remembers, goodwife Stapleyes went along wth her all the way till they came at ye gallowes. Further this deponent saith, that Mr. Jones some time since that Knapps wife was condemned, did tell her, and that wth a very cherefull countenance & blessing God for it, that Knapps wife had cleered one in ye towne, & said you know who I meane sister Staplyes, blessed be God for it."

Staplies' wife was a character. She was "a light woman" from the night of her memorable ride with Tom Tash, to Jemeaco, Long Island, to the suspicion of herself as a witch, and the "repairing" of her name by Thomas' lawsuit, and her own indictment for familiarity with Satan some years later. That she had many of the traditional witch qualities, and was something of a gymnast and hypnotist, is written in the vivid recollections of Tash's experience with her. This was his account of it on oath thirty years after:

"John Tash aged about sixty four or thareabouts saith he being at Master Laueridges at Newtown on Long Island aboutt thirty year since Goodman Owen and Goody Owin desired me to goe with Thomas Stapels wiffe of Fairfield to Jemeaco on Long Island to the hous of George Woolsy and as we war going along we cam to a durty slow and thar the hors blundred in the slow and I mistrusted that she the said Goody Stapels was off the hors and I was troubiled in my mind very much soe as I cam back I thought I would tak better noatis how it was and when I cam to the slow abovesaid I put on the hors prity sharp and then I put my hand behind me and felt for her and she was not upon the hors and as soon as we war out of the slow she was on the hors behind me boath going and coming and when I cam home I told thes words to Master Leveredg that she was a light woman as I judged and I am redy to give oath to this when leagaly caled tharunto as witnes my hand.

his "John+Tash mark

"Grenwich July 12, 1692.

"John Tash hath given oath to his testimony abovesaid

"Before me John Renels Comessener."

And Mistress Staplies had other qualities, always potent in small communities to invite criticism and dislike. She was a shrewd and shrewish woman, impatient of some of the Puritan social standards and of the laws of everyday life. She openly condemned certain common moralities, was reckless in criticism of her neighbors, and quarreled with Ludlow about some church matters.

It is evident from the testimonies that Staplies was on both sides as to the guilt of goodwife Knapp, and when rumor and suspicion began to point to herself as a mischief-maker and busybody in witchcraft matters, to divert attention from his wife and set a backfire to the sweep of public opinion, Thomas sued Ludlow, and despite his strong and clear defense as shown on the record evidence, the court in his absence awarded damages against him for defamation and for charging Staplies' wife with going on "in a tract of lying," "in reparation of his wife's name" as the judgment reads. Mistress Staplies did not grow in grace, or in the graces of her neighbors, since some years later she was indicted for witchcraft, tried, and acquitted with others, at Fairfield, in 1692. [J]

[J] See *Historical Note*, p. 161.

CHAPTER XI

"The planters of New England were Englishmen, not exempt from English prejudices in favor of English institutions, laws and usages ... They had not been taught to question the wisdom or the humanity of English criminal law. They were as unconscious of its barbarism, as were the parliaments which had enacted or the courts which dispensed it." *Blue Laws, True and False* (p. 15), J. HAMMOND TRUMBULL.

"It would seem a marvellous panic, this that shook the rugged reasoners in its iron grasp, and led to such insanity as this displayed toward Alse Young, did we not know that it was but the result of a normal inhuman law confirmed by a belief in the divine, the direct legacy of England, the unquestionable utterance of Church and State." *One Blank of Windsor*, ANNIE ELIOT TRUMBULL.

This brief review of witchcraft in some of its historical aspects, of its spread to the New England colonies, of its rise and suppression in the Connecticut towns, with the citations from the original records which admit no challenge of the facts, may be aptly closed by what is believed to be a complete list of the Connecticut witchcraft cases, authenticated by conclusive evidence of time, place, incident, and circumstance.

Some minor questions may be put, or kept in controversy, as one writer or another, who regards history as a matter of opinion, not of fact, and relying on tradition or hearsay evidence or on superficial investigation, gives a place to guesswork instead of truth, to historical conceits instead of historical verities.

A RECORD OF THE MEN AND WOMEN WHO CAME UNDER SUSPICION OR ACCUSATION OF WITCHCRAFT IN CONNECTICUT, AND WHAT BEFELL THEM.

Herein are written the names of all persons in anywise involved in the witchcraft delusion in Connecticut, with the consequences to them in indictments, trials, convictions, executions, or in banishment, exile, warnings, reprieves, or acquittals, so far as made known in any tradition, document, public or private record, to this time.

MARY JOHNSON. Windsor, 1647.

There is no documentary or other evidence to show that Mary Johnson was executed for witchcraft in Windsor in 1647. The charge rests on an entry in Governor Winthrop's *Journal*, "One ---- of Windsor arraigned and executed at Hartford for a witch." WINTHROP'S *History of New England* (Savage, 2: 374).

No importance would have attached to this statement, which bears no date and does not give the name or sex of the condemned, had not Dr. Savage in his annotations of the *Journal* (2: 374) asserted that it was "the first instance of the delusion in New England," and without warrant added, "Perhaps there was sense enough early in the colony to destroy the record."

In all discussions of this matter, it has been assumed or conceded (in the absence of any positive proof), by such eminent critics and scholars as Drake, Fiske, Poole, Hoadley, Stiles, and others, that Winthrop's note was based on rumor or hearsay, or that it related to the later conviction and execution of a woman of the same name, next noted, and the errors as to person, time, and place might easily have been made.

MARY JOHNSON. Wethersfield, 1648.

This Mary Johnson left a definite record. It is written in broad lines in the dry-as-dust chronicles of the time. Cotton Mather embalmed the tragedy in his *Magnalia*.

"There was one Mary Johnson tryd at Hartford in this countrey, upon an indictment of 'familiarity with the devil,' and was found guilty thereof, chiefly upon her own confession."

"And she dyd in a frame extreamly to the satisfaction of them that were spectators of it." *Magnalia Christi Americana* (6: 7).

At a session of the Particular Court held in Hartford, August 21, 1646, Mary Johnson for thievery was sentenced to be presently whipped, and to be brought forth a month hence at Wethersfield, and there whipped. The whipping post, even in those days, did not prove a means to repentance and reformation, since at a session of the same court, December 7, 1648, the jury found a bill of indictment against Mary Johnson, that by her own confession she was guilty of familiarity with the devil.

That she was condemned and executed seems certain (it being assumed that Mary and Elizabeth Johnson were one and the same person, both Christian names appearing in the record), since at a session of the General Court, May 21, 1650, the prison-keeper's charges for her imprisonment were allowed and ordered paid "out of her estate."

A pathetic incident attaches to this case. A child to this poor woman was "borne in the prison," who was bound out until he became twenty-one years of age, to Nathaniel Rescew, to whom £15 were paid according to the mother's promise to him, he having engaged himself "to meinteine and well educate her sonne." *Colonial Records of Connecticut* (I,143: 171: 209-22-26-32).

THE FIRST EXECUTION FOR WITCHCRAFT IN NEW ENGLAND

A secret long kept made known – Winthrop's journal entry probably correct – Tradition and surmise make place for historical certainty – The evidence of an eyewitness – A notable service.

ALSE YOUNG. Windsor, 1647.

"May 26. 47 Alse Young was hanged." MATTHEW GRANT'S *Diary*.

"The first entry (the executions of Carrington and his wife being next mentioned) supplies the name of the 'One (blank) of Windsor arraigned and executed at Hartford for a witch'—the first known execution for witchcraft in New England. I have found no mention elsewhere of this Alse Young." J. HAMMOND TRUMBULL'S *Observation on Grant's Entry*.

"Who then was the 'witch' with whose execution Connecticut stepped into the dark shadow of persecution? She has been called Mary Johnson, but no Mary Johnson has been identified as this earliest victim. Whose is that pathetic figure shrinking in the twilight of that early record? We could think of her with no less kindly compassion could we give a name to the unhappy victim of the misread Word of God, who was led forth to a death stripped of dignity as of consolation: who to an ignorance and credulity, brought from an old world and not yet sifted out by the enlightenment and experience of a new, yielded up her perhaps miserable but unforfeited life. Here is the note which in all probability establishes the identity of the One of Windsor arraigned and executed as a witch—'May 26, 47 Alse Young was hanged.'" *"One Blank" of Windsor* (Courant Literary Section, 12, 3, 1904), ANNIE ELIOT TRUMBULL.

Matthew Grant came over with the Dorchester men from the Bay Colony in 1635, and settled in Windsor, Connecticut, where he lived until his death there in 1683.

He was a land surveyor, and the town clerk, a close observer of men and their public and private affairs, and kept a careful record of current events in a "crabbed, eccentric but by no means entirely illegible hand" during the long years of his sojourn in the "Lord's Waste."

It has been surmised for several years—but without confirmation—and credited by the highest authorities in Connecticut colonial history, and known only to one of them, that Grant's manuscript diary contained the significant historical note as to the fate of Alse Young. It waited two centuries and more for its true interpreter, as did Wolcott's cipher notes of Hooker's famous sermon, and there it is, "not made on the decorous pages which memorize the saints," Brookes, Hooker, Warham, Reyner, Hanford, and Huit, "but scrawled on the inside of the cover, where it might be the sinner might escape detection."

In the publication of Grant's note Miss Trumbull has rendered a great service in the settlement of a disputed question, in the correction of errors, in fixing the priority of the outbreak between Massachusetts and Connecticut; and in the new light shining through this revelation stands Alse, glorified with the qualities of youth, of gentleness, of innocence; and the story of her going to the unholy sacrifice on that fateful May morning more than two and a half centuries ago is told with exquisite tenderness and pathos.

Confirmation of the truth of Grant's entry is given by the scholarly historian of Windsor, Dr. Stiles, who says in his history of that ancient town:

"We know that a John Youngs, [?] bought land in Windsor of William Hubbard in 1641—which he sold in 1649—and thereafter disappears from record. He may have been the husband or father of 'Achsah'[?] the witch; if so, it would be most natural that he and his family should leave Windsor." STILES' *History of Windsor* (pp. 444-450).

JOHN and JOAN CARRINGTON. Wethersfield, 1651.

They were indicted at a court held February 20, 1651, Governor John Haynes and Edward Hopkins being present, with other magistrates; and they were found guilty on March 6, 1651. Both were executed. *Records Particular Court* (2: 17). [Dr. Hoadley's note in this case: "Mr. Trumbull (Dr. J. Hammond Trumbull) told me he had a record of execution in these cases. I suppose he referred to the diary of Matthew Grant."] The entry of the execution appears in Grant's *Diary*, after the note as to Alse Young. *One Blank of Windsor*, TRUMBULL.

LYDIA GILBERT. Windsor, 1654.

October 3, 1651, Henry Stiles of Windsor was killed by the accidental discharge of a gun in the hands of Thomas Allyn, also of Windsor. An inquest was held, and Thomas was indicted in the following December. He plead guilty, and at the trial the jury found the fact to be "homicide by misadventure." Thomas was fined £20 for his "sinful neglect and careless carriage," and put under a bond of £10, for good behavior for a year. *Records Particular Court* (2: 29-57).

But witchcraft was abroad, and its tools and emissaries more than two years afterwards fastened suspicion of this death by clear accident, on Lydia Gilbert, it being charged that "thou hast of late years, or still dost give entertainment to Sathan ... and by his helpe hast killed the body of Henry Styles, besides other witchcrafts."

She was indicted and tried in September or November, 1654, and "Ye party above mentioned is found guilty of witchcraft by ye jury." Her fate is not written in any known record, but the late Honorable S.O. Griswold, a recognized authority on early colonial history in Windsor, says that as the result of a close examination of the record, "I think the reasonable probability is that she was hanged." *Records Particular Court* (2: 51); STILE'S *History of Windsor* (pp. 169, 444-450).

GOODY BASSETT. Stratford, 1651. Executed.

"The Gouernor, Mr. Cullick, and Mr. Clarke are desired to goe downe to Stratford to keepe courte uppon the tryall of Goody Bassett for her life"—May, 1651. "Because goodwife Bassett when she was condemned" (probably on her own confession, as in the Greensmith case). *Colonial Records of Connecticut* (1: 220); *New Haven Colonial Records* (2: 77-88).

GOODWIFE KNAPP. Fairfield, 1653. Executed.

"After goodwife Knapp was executed, as soon as she was cut downe." *New Haven Colonial Records* (1: 81).

Full account in previous chapter.

ELIZABETH GODMAN. New Haven, 1655. Acquitted.

Elizabeth was released from prison September 4, 1655, with a reprimand and warning by the court. *New Haven Town Records* (2: 174, 179); *New Haven Colonial Records* (2: 29, 151).

Account in previous chapter.

NICHOLAS BAYLEY and WIFE. New Haven, 1655. Acquitted.

Nicholas and his wife, after several appearances in court on account of a suspicion of witchcraft, and for various other offenses—among them, lying and filthy speeches by the wife—were advised to remove from the colony. They took the advice.

WILLIAM MEAKER. New Haven, 1657. Accused acquitted.

Thomas Mullener was always in trouble. He was a chronic litigant. His many contentions are noted at length in the court records. Among other things he made up his mind that his pigs were bewitched, so "he did cut of the tayle and eare of one and threw into the fire," "said it was a meanes used in England by some people to finde out witches," and in the light of this porcine sacrifice he charged his neighbor William Meaker with the bewitching. Meaker promptly brought an action of defamation, but Mullener became involved in other controversies and "miscarriages," to the degree that he was advised to remove out of the place, and put under bonds for good behavior; and Meaker, probably feeling himself vindicated, dropped his suit. *New Haven Colonial Records* (2: 224).

ELIZABETH GARLICK. Easthampton, 1658. Acquitted.

Records Particular Court (2 :113); *Colonial Records of Connecticut* (1: 573); STILES' *History of Windsor* (p. 735).

Account in previous chapter.

NICHOLAS and MARGARET JENNINGS. Saybrook, 1661.

Jury disagreed.

The major part of the jury found Nicholas guilty, but the rest only strongly suspected him, and as to Margaret, some found her guilty, and the others suspected her to be guilty. It is probable that the Jennings were under inquiry when, at a session of the General Court at Hartford, June 15, 1659, it was recorded that "Mr. Willis is requested to goe downe to Sea Brook, to assist ye Maior in examininge the suspitions about witchery, and to act therin as may be requisite." *Records Particular Court* (2: 160-3); *Colonial Records of Connecticut* (1: 338).

1662-63 was a notable year in the history of witchcraft in Connecticut. It marked the last execution for the crime within the commonwealth, and thirty years before the outbreak at Salem.

NATHANIEL GREENSMITH and REBECCA his WIFE. Hartford, 1662. Both executed.

Account in previous chapter. *Records Particular Court* (2: 182); *Memorial History Hartford County* (1: 274); *Connecticut Magazine* (November 1899, pp. 557-561).

MARY SANFORD. Hartford, 1662. Convicted June 13, 1662. Executed.

Records Particular Court (2: 174-175); HOADLEY'S *Record Witchcraft Trials.*

ANDREW SANFORD. Hartford, 1662. No indictment.

Records Particular Court (2: 174-175); HOADLEY'S *Record Witchcraft Trials.*

JUDITH VARLETT (VARLETH). Hartford, 1662. Arrested; released.

It will be recalled that Rebecca Greensmith in her confession, among other things, said that Mrs. Judith Varlett told her that she (Varlett) "was much troubled wth ye Marshall Jonath: Gilbert & cried, & she sayd if it lay in her power she would doe him a mischief, or what hurt shee could."

Judith must have indulged in other indiscretions of association or of speech, since she soon fell under suspicion of witchcraft, and was put under arrest and imprisoned. But she had a powerful friend at court (who, despite his many contentions and intrigues, commanded the attention of the Connecticut authorities), in the person of her brother-in-law Peter Stuyvesant, then bearing the title and office of "Captain General and Commander-in-Chief of Amsterdam In New Netherland, now called New York, and the Dutch West India Islands." It was doubtless due to his intercession in a letter of October 13, 1662, that she was released.

The letter:

"To the Honorable Deputy Governour & Court of
"Magistracy att Harafort. (Oct. 1662)

"Honoured and Worthy Srs. –

"By this occasion of me Brother in Lawe (beinge necessitated to make a Second Voyage for ayde his distressed sister Judith Varleth jmprisoned as we are jmformed, uppon pretend accusation of wicherye we Realy Beleeve and out her wel known education Life Conversation & profession of faith, wee dear assure that shee is jnnocent of Such a horrible Crimen, & wherefor j doubt not hee will now, as formerly finde jour dhonnours favour and ayde for the jnnocent). *Ye Ld Stephesons Letter* (C.B. 2: doc. 1).

MARY BARNES. Farmington, 1662. Convicted January 6. Probably executed. *Records Particular Court* (2: 184).

WILLIAM AYRES and GOODY AYRES his Wife. Hartford, 1662. Arrested. Fled from the colony.

ELIZABETH SEAGER. Hartford, 1662. Convicted; discharged.

Goody Seager probably deserved all that came to her in trials and punishment. She was one of the typical characters in the early communities upon whom distrust and dislike and suspicion inevitably fell. Exercising witch powers was one of her more reputable qualities. She was indicted for blasphemy, adultery, and witchcraft at various times, was convicted of adultery, and found guilty of witchcraft in June, 1665. She owed her escape from hanging to a finding of the Court of Assistants that the jury's verdict did not legally answer to the indictment, and she was set "free from further suffering or imprisonment." *Records County Court* (3. 5. 52), *Colonial Records of Connecticut* (2: 531); *Rhode Island Colonial Records* (2: 388).

JAMES WALKLEY. Hartford, 1662. Arrested. Fled to Rhode Island.

KATHERINE HARRISON. Wethersfield, 1669. Convicted; discharged.

See account in previous chapter. *Records Court of, Assistants* (I, 1-7); *Colonial Records of Connecticut* (2: 118, 132); *Doc. History New York* (4th ed., 4: 87).

NICHOLAS DESBOROUGH. Hartford, 1683. Suspicioned.

Desborough was a landowner in Hartford, having received a grant of fifty acres for his services in the Pequot war. He owes his enrollment in the hall of fame to Cotton Mather, who was so self-satisfied with his efforts in "Relating the wonders of the invisible world in preternatural occurrences" that in his pedantic exuberance he put in a learned sub-title: "Miranda cano, sed sunt credenda" (The themes I sing are marvelous, yet true).

Fourteen examples were chosen for the "Thaumatographia Pneumatica," as "remarkable histories" of molestations from evil spirits, and Mather said of them, "that no reasonable man in this whole country ever did question them."

Desborough stands in place as the "fourth example." No case more clearly illustrates the credulity that neutralized common sense in strong men. It was a case of abstraction, or theft, or mistaken thrift. A "chest of cloaths" was missing. The owner, instead of going to law, found his remedy "in things beyond the course of nature," and he and his friends with "nimble hands" pelted Desborough's house, and himself when abroad, with stones, turves, and corncobs, and finally some of his property was burned by a fire "in an unknown way kindled." Is it not enough to note that Mather closes this wondrous tale of the spiritual molestations with the very human explanation that "upon the restoring of the cloaths, the trouble ceased"?

ELIZABETH CLAWSON. Fairfield, 1692. Acquitted. Account in previous chapter.

MARY and HANNAH HARVEY. Fairfield, 1692. Jury found no bill.

GOODY MILLER. Fairfield, 1692. Acquitted.

MARY STAPLIES. Fairfield, 1692. Jury found no bill. Account in previous chapter.

MERCY DISBOROUGH. Fairfield, 1692. Convicted; reprieved. Account in previous chapter.

HUGH CROTIA. Stratford, 1693. Jury found no bill. Account in previous chapter. *C. & D.* (Vol. I,185).

WINIFRED BENHAM SENIOR and JUNIOR. Wallingford, 1697. Acquitted.

They were mother and daughter (twelve or thirteen years old), tried at Hartford and acquitted in August, 1697; indicted on new complaints in October, 1697, but the jury returned on the bill, "Ignoramus." *Records Court of Assistants* (1: 74, 77).

SARAH SPENCER. Colchester, 1724. Accused. Damages 1s.

Even a certificate of the minister as to her religion and virtue, could not free Sarah from a reputation as a witch. And when Elizabeth (and how many Connecticut witches bore that name) Ackley accused her of "riding and pinching," and James Ackley, her husband, made threats, Sarah sued them for a fortune in those days, £500 damages, and got judgment for £5, with costs. The Ackleys appealed, and at the trial the jury awarded Sarah damages of ls., and also stated that they found the Ackleys not insane—a clear demonstration that the mental condition of witchcraft accusers was taken account of in the later and saner times.

NORTON. Bristol, 1768. Suspicioned. No record.

"On the mountain," probably Fall mountain in Bristol, the antics of a young woman named Norton, who accused her aunt of putting a bridle on her and driving her through the air to witch meetings in Albany, caused a commotion among the virtuous people. Deacon Dutton's ox was torn apart by an invisible agent, and unseen hands brought new ailments to the residents there, pinched them and stuck red hot pins into them. Elder Wildman set out to exorcise the evil spirit, but became so terrorized that he called for help, and one of his posse of assistants was scared into convulsions. This case may be counted among the last, perhaps the last traditions of the strange delusion which aforetime filled the hills and valleys of Quohnectacut with its baleful light. *Memorial History Hartford County* (2: 51).

ROLL OF NAMES

ALSE YOUNG	1647
MARY JOHNSON	1648
JOHN CARRINGTON	1650-51
JOAN CARRINGTON	1650-71
GOODY BASSETT	1651
GOODWIFE KNAPP	1653
LYDIA GILBERT	1654
ELIZABETH GODMAN	1655
NICHOLAS BAYLY	1655
GOODWIFE BAYLY	1655
WILLIAM MEAKER	1657
ELIZABETH GARLICK	1658
NICHOLAS JENNINGS	1661
MARGARET JENNINGS	1661
NATHANIEL GREENSMITH	1662
REBECCA GREENSMITH	1662
MARY SANFORD	1662
ANDREW SANFORD	1662
GOODY AYRES	1662
KATHERINE PALMER	1662
JUDITH VARLETT	1662
JAMES WALKLEY	1662
MARY BARNES	1662-63
ELIZABETH SEAGER	1666
KATHERINE HARRISON	1669
NICHOLAS DISBOROUGH	1683
MARY STAPLIES	1692
MERCY DISBOROUGH	1692
ELIZABETH CLAWSON	1692
MARY HARVEY	1692
HANNAH HARVEY	1692
GOODY MILLER	1692

HUGH CROTIA	1693
WINIFRED BENHAM, SENR.	1697
WINIFRED BENHAM, JUNR.	1697
SARAH SPENCER	1724
---- NORTON	1768

What of those men and women to whom justice in their time was meted out, in this age of reason, of religious enlightenment, liberty, and catholicity, when witchcraft has lost its mystery and power, when intelligence reigns, and the Devil works his will in other devious ways and in a more attractive guise?

They were the victims of delusion, not of dishonor, of a perverted theology fed by moral aberrations, of a fanaticism which never stopped to reason, and halted at no sacrifice to do God's service; and they were all done to death, or harried into exile, disgrace, or social ostracism, through a mistaken sense of religious duty: but they stand innocent of deep offense and only guilty in the eye of the law written in the Word of God, as interpreted and enforced by the forefathers who wrought their condemnation, and whose religion made witchcraft a heinous sin, and whose law made it a heinous crime.

Is the contrast in human experience, between the servitude to credulity and superstition in 1647-97 and the deliverance from it of this day, any wider than between the ironclad theology of that and of later times, and the challenge to it, and its diabolical logic, of yesterday, which marks a new era in denominational creeds, in religious beliefs, and their expression?

Jonathan Edwards, in his famous sermon at Enfield in 1741, on "Sinners in the hands of an Angry God," was inspired to say to the impenitent: "The God that holds you over the pit of hell, much as one holds a spider or some loathsome insect over the fire, abhors you and is dreadfully provoked; His wrath toward you burns like fire; He looks upon you as worthy of nothing else but to be cast into the fire; He is of purer eyes than to bear to have you in His sight; you are 10,000 times so abominable in His eyes as the most hateful and venomous serpent is in ours.... Instead of one how many is it likely will remember this discourse in hell! And it would be a wonder if some that are now present should not be in hell in a very short time—before this year is out. And it would be no wonder if some persons, that now sit here in some seats of this meeting-house, in health and quiet, and secure, should be there before to-morrow morning." One hundred and sixty-three years later, Rev. Dr. Samuel T. Carter, a godly minister of the same faith, "a heretic who is no heretic," stood before the presbytery of Nassau, was invited to remain in the Presbyterian communion, and yet said this of the doctrine of Edwards, as written in the *Westminster Confession*: "In God's name and Christ's name it is not true. There is no such God as the God of the confession. There is no such world as the world of the confession. There is no such eternity as the eternity of the confession.... This world so full of flowers and sunshine and the laughter of children is not a cursed lost world, and the 'endless torment' of the confession is not God's, nor Christ's, nor the Bible's idea of future punishment."

What should constitute the true faith of a Christian, and set him apart from his fellowmen in duties and observances, was one of the crucial questions in the everyday life of the early New England colonists, and the hanging and discipline of witches was one of its necessary incidents.

It was the same spirit of intolerance and of religious animosity that was written in the treatment of the Quakers and Baptists at Boston; in the experience of Roger Williams and Anne Hutchinson; and of "The Rogerenes" in Connecticut, for "profanation of the Sabbath," told in a chapter of forgotten history.

In the sunlight of the later revelation, is not the present judgment of the men and women of those far off times, "when the wheel of prayer was in perpetual motion," when fear and superstition and the wrath of an angry God ruled the strongest minds, truly interpreted in the solemn afterthoughts which the poet ascribes to the magistrate and minister at the grave of Giles Corey?

HATHORNE
"This is the Potter's Field. Behold the fate
Of those who deal in witchcrafts, and when questioned,
Refuse to plead their guilt or innocence,
And stubbornly drag death upon themselves.
MATHER

"Those who lie buried in the Potter's Field
Will rise again as surely as ourselves
That sleep in honored graves with epitaphs;
And this poor man whom we have made a victim,
Hereafter will be counted as a martyr."
The New England Tragedies.

HISTORICAL NOTE

ROGER LUDLOW

The Connecticut historians to a very recent date, in ignorance of the facts, and despite his notable services of twenty-four years to the colonies, left Ludlow to die in obscurity in Virginia or elsewhere, and some of the traditions, based on no record or other evidence, have been recently repeated. It is therefore proper to state here in few words who Ludlow was, what he did both in Massachusetts and Connecticut, and after his "return into England" in 1654.

Ludlow came of an ancient English family, which gave to history in his own time and generation such illustrious kinsmen as Sir Henry Ludlow, a member of the Long Parliament and one of the Puritan leaders, and Sir Edmund Ludlow, member of Parliament, Lieutenant-General under Cromwell, member of the court at King Charles' trial, and whom Macaulay named "the most illustrious saviour of a mighty race of men, the judges of a king, the founders of a republic."

In May, 1630, Ludlow came to Massachusetts, as one of the Assistants under the charter of "The Governor and company of Massachusetts Bay in New England."

His services in the Bay Colony from 1630-35 ranged from the duties of a magistrate in the Great Charter Court to those of the high office of Deputy Governor. The quality of that service is written in a bare statement of his various offices—surveyor, negotiator of the Pequot treaty, colonel ex officio, auditor of Governor Winthrop's accounts, superintendent of fortifications, military commissioner, member of the General Court, Deputy Governor when Thomas Dudley was Governor; and he was always one of the foremost men in civil, political, and social affairs, to the day of his departure to "the valley of the long river,"—a day of good fortune for Connecticut.

When Massachusetts established church membership as the condition of suffrage,—and radical differences of opinion on other matters arose,—it marked the culmination of a set purpose of some of her ablest men to remove from her jurisdiction, among whom Hooker, Ludlow, and Haynes were the most notable. The General Court created a commission to govern Connecticut for a year, and made Ludlow its chief. He came to the new land of promise with the Dorchester men, and settled in Windsor in 1635-36.

What he did in the nineteen years of his residence at Windsor and Fairfield is epitomized in a brief summary of the duties and honors to which he was called by his fellowmen:

Chief of the Massachusetts commission and the first Governor, de facto; organizer and chief magistrate of the first court; writer of the earliest laws; president of the court which declared war against the Pequots; framer of the Fundamental Orders—the Constitution of 1639—which embodied the great principles of government by the people propounded and elucidated by the illustrious Thomas Hooker, in his letter to Governor Winthrop, and in his famous sermon; compiler, at the request of the General Court, of the *Body of Lawes*, the *Code of 1650*; commissioner on important state matters; commissioner for the United Colonies; founder and defender of Fairfield; patriot, jurist, statesman.

Ludlow left Connecticut in 1654, not to die in obscurity as the earlier writers imagined, but to serve abroad for several years in positions of honor and distinction.

Cromwell invited him to return, as he did many of the leading Puritans in New England, and appointed him a commissioner for the administration of justice in Dublin; also to serve with the chief justice of the upper bench and other distinguished lawyers, to determine all the claims to the forfeited Irish lands, and at last as a Master in Chancery.

Ten years Ludlow served in these important stations; and at his death, probably in 1664, he was buried in St. Michael's churchyard in Dublin, with his wife—a sister of Governor John Endicott—and other members of his family. [K]

[K] *Roger Ludlow – The Colonial Lawmaker*—TAYLOR.

BIBLIOGRAPHICAL NOTE

Some of the authorities and records in witchcraft literature consulted in the writing of this essay are here cited for reference and information:

Connecticut Archives: *Wyllys Papers, Original Witchcraft Depositions*; Records: *General Court, Particular Court, Court of Assistants, County Court, Colonial Boundaries, Crimes and Misdemeanors, Connecticut Colonial, New Haven Colonial, Hartford Probate, New Haven Town; Magnolia Christi Americana* (MATHER); MATTHEW GRANT'S *Diary* (TRUMBULL'S *Observations*) *Courant Literary Section*, 12-3-1904; HOADLEY'S *Witchcraft Trials and Notes* (Manuscript); WINTHROP'S *History of New England;* STILES' *History of Windsor; Blue Laws, True and False* (TRUMBULL); PERKINS' *Discourse; The Literature of Witchcraft* (BURR); *Hammurabi's Code; Cent. Mag.*, June, 1903; BLACKSTONE'S *Commentaries; A Tale of the Witches* (STONE); LECKY'S *Rationalism in Europe; The Witch Persecutions* (BURR); Encyc. Articles ("Witchcraft"): *Britannica, Americana, International, Chambers', Johnson's; Connecticut: Origin of her Courts and Laws* (HAMERSLEY); BARBER'S *Connecticut Historical Collections;* SCHENCK'S *Fairfield; Connecticut as a Colony and State* (MORGAN et al.); *The House of the Seven Gables* (HAWTHORNE); LATIMER'S *Salem;* JOHNSTON'S *Nathan Hale; Connecticut History* (TRUMBULL); UPHAM'S *Salem Witchcraft; Conn. Mag.*, Nov., 1899; Dalton's *Justice; Mem. Hist, of Boston; Mem. Hist, of Hartford County*; Palfrey's *New England; Historic Towns of New England* (Latimer); *Giles Corey of the Salem Farms* (Longfellow); *New France and New England* (Fiske); Scott's *Demonology and Witchcraft;* Lowell's "Witchcraft" (*Among My Books*); Whitmore's *Colonial Laws;* Drake's *Witchcraft Delusion in New England;* Fowler's *Salem Witchcraft;* Hutchinson's *Hist, of Massachus-*

etts Bay; Larned's *Hist, of Ready Reference* (Mass.); Howe's *Puritan Republic*; Goodwin's *Pilgrim Republic*; Merejkowski's *Romance of Leonardo da Vinci*; Bulwer's *Last Days of Pompeii*; Weyman's *The Long Night*; Crockett's *The Black Douglas*; Lea's *Hist, of the Inquisition; Scarlet Letter* (Hawthorne); *A Case of Witchcraft in Connecticut* (Hoadley); *Witches in Connecticut* (Bliss); *Historical Discourses* (Bacon); *History of Wethersfield* (Stiles); *History of Long Island* (Thompson), *Witchcraft in Boston* (Poole); *Literature of Witchcraft in New England* (Winsor); *Witchcraft and Second Sight in the Scottish Highlands* (Campbell); *Witchhunter in the Bookshops* (Burr); *Epidemic Delusions* (Carpenter); *History of New England* (Neal); *History of Colonization of U.S.* (Bancroft); *Salem Witchcraft* (Fowler); Bouvier's *Law Dic.; Witchcraft in Connecticut* (Livermore); *Witchcraft in Salem Village*, 1692 (Nevins); *History of Stratford and Bridgeport* (Orcutt); *Bench and Bar* (Adams); Conway's *Demonology and Devil-lore; Domestic and Social Life in Colonial Times* (Warner); *Nat. Mag.* Nov. 15, 1891.

Index

A

Allyn, John 44, 51-56, 65-67, 71, 84, 106, 109, 117
Allyn, Thomas 148
Ashley, Jonathan 117
Austen, Thomas 103
Ayres, Goody 152, 157
Ayres, William 152

B

Baldwin, Goodwife 133, 137
Ball, Allen 94
Bankes, John 126
Barlow, Goodwife 135

Barlow, John 65
Barnard, Bartholomew 117
Barnes, Mary 152, 157
Bassett, Goody 130, 148, 156
Bates, Sarah 104
Bayley, Goodwife 149, 156
Bayley, Nicholas 149, 156
Belden, Samuel 51
Bell, Jonathan 44, 105-107, 110, 113
Benham, Winifred, Jr. and Sr. 155, 157
Benit, Elizabeth 67, 70
Benit, Thomas 67, 71
Benit, Thomas, Jr. 70
Birdsall, Goody 120
Bishop, Bridgett ix
Bishop, Ebenezer 108
Bishop, Edward ix
Bowman, Nathanael 117
Bracy, Thomas 49
Branch, Catherine 65, 103-104, 108-116
Brewster, Elizabeth 131
Brewster, Mary 132
Brundish, Bethia 134
Bryan, Ensign 126, 129
Bulkeley, Rev. Gershom 57
Bull, Joseph 117
Burr, Abigail 43
Burr, John 110, 119
Burr, Sarah 43
Buxstum, Clement 113

C

Carrington, Joan 38, 145, 147, 156
Carrington, John viii, 38, 145, 147, 156
Carter, Dr. Samuel T. 159

Chester, Stephen	117
Clarke, Mr.	38, 148
Clarke, Henry	50, 52, 53
Clarke, William	51
Clawson, Elizabeth	44, 63, 101-116, 154, 157
Clawson, Stephen	101
Cole, Ann	97
Collins, Samuel	117
Comstock, Christopher	133
Corey, Giles	15, 27
Corwin, George	ix
Corwin, Jonathan	27
Cross, Abigail	104
Cross, Nathanael	104
Crotia, Hugh	viii, 117-119, 155, 157
Cullick, Mr.	38, 56, 148

D

Davenport, Rev. John	85, 122, 125-128
Davis, Goody	120
Desborough, Nicholas	153, 157
Dickinson, Joseph	50
Disborough, Mercy	15, 44, 62-78, 154, 157
Disborough, Thomas	63, 65
Duning, Benjamin	65

E

Eaton, Theophilus	85, 125
Edwards, Goody	120
Edwards, Jonathan	158
Eliot, Joseph	76, 78

F

Finch, Abraham 107
Fowler, William 125, 138
Francis, Joane 53
Fyler, Walt. 85

G

Gardiner, Lion 119
Garlick, Elizabeth 119-121, 150, 156
Garlick, Joshua 119
Garney, Joseph 101
Garrett, Daniel 80
Garrett, Margaret 80
Gedney, Bartholomew 27
Gibbons, William 117
Gilbert, Lydia 148, 156
Gillett, Cornelius 117
Godfree, Ann 70
Godman, Elizabeth 85-96, 149, 156
Gold, Nathan 110, 119
Goodyear, Stephen 85-89, 92, 93
Gould, Goodwife 139
Grant, Matthew 146-147
Graves, John 52
Greensmith, Nathaniel 96-100, 151, 156
Greensmith, Rebecca 96-100, 151, 156
Grey, Henry 68, 69, 70
Griswold, Edward 38
Griswold, Michael 59
Grummon, John 70

H

Hale, Mary 54
Halliberch, Thomas 66
Hand, Goody 121
Harrison, Katherine 47-61, 153, 157
Hart, Stephen 38, 81
Harvey, Hannah 115, 154, 157
Harvey, Mary 154, 157
Hathorne, John 27
Haynes, John 38, 97, 98, 147
Heyden, Daniel 117
Hollister, Mr. 38
Holly, Samuel 109
Hooker, Thomas 162
Hopkins, Edward 38, 147
Hopkins, Matthew 21
Howard, Abigail 43
Howell, Goodwife 119
Hubbard, Elizabeth ix
Hull, Rebecca 133
Hull, Cornelius 133

J

Jennings, Margaret 150, 156
Jennings, Nicholas 150, 156
Jesop, Edward 63
Joanes, William 117
Johnson, Jacob 53
Johnson, Mary 35, 143, 144, 156
Jones, Martha 35
Jones, William 40
Judd, Theo. 38

K

Kecham, Sarah 103
Kelsey, Stephen 117
Knapp, Goodwife 109, 122-141, 156, 176

L

Lamberton, Desire 93
Lamberton, Elizabeth 86, 90
Lamberton, Hannah 86, 90
Langton, Joseph 117
Leawis, Will. 38
Leete, William 47, 125
Lewis, Mercy ix
Lockwood, Deborah 133
Lockwood, Robert 132
Lockwood, Susan 124, 131, 132, 136, 138
Loomis, Jonathan 117
Loomis, Nathanael 117
Ludlow, Roger 123, 125-129, 161-163
Lyon, Thomas 136, 138

M

Mansfield, Moses 117
Marsh, John 117
Mason, John 47
Mather, Cotton 28-34, 153
Meaker, William 149, 156
Migat, Mrs. 82
Miller, Goody 154, 157
Milton, Daniel 38

More, John 38
Montague, Richard 51
Mullener, Thomas 149
Mygatt, Joseph 117

N

Newell, Samuel 117
Newton, Thomas 27
North, Joseph 117
Norton 155, 157

O

Odell, Goodwife 124, 131, 135

P

Palmer, Katherine 157
Pantry, John 117
Pell, Luce 124, 130, 135, 138
Penoir, Lydia 112
Phelps, Abraham 117
Phelps, Mr. 38
Pitkin, William 78, 117
Pratt, Daniel 81
Pratt, John 38
Purdy, Goodwife 124, 135
Putnam, Ann ix, 30

R

Renels, John 141
Richards, John 27
Russel, William 120

S

Saltonstall, Nathl. 27
Sanford, Andrew 151, 157
Sanford, Mary 151, 156
Seager, Elizabeth 80-85, 152, 157
Selleck, David 108, 114
Selleck, Jonathan 106, 107, 110, 116
Sergeant, Peter 27
Sewall, Samuel 27
Shervington, Thomas 133, 138
Sherwood, Isaac 64
Sherwood, Mistress Thomas 124, 128, 135, 139
Slawson, Elezer 113
Smith, Elizabeth 56
Smith, Philip 51
Smith, Samuel 38, 50, 52, 53, 66
Spencer, Sarah 155, 157
Stanly, Caleb 117
Stanly, Nath. 78, 117
Staplies, Mary 125-141, 154, 157
Staplies, Thomas 125, 126
Steele, James 117
Sterne, Robert 81, 84
Stiles, Henry 148
Stirg, Joseph 66
Stoughton, John 117
Stoughton, William 27, ix

T

Tailecote, Mr.	38
Tash, John	140, 141
Tompson, J.	129, 135
Treat, Robert	48, 62, 117
Trumbull, J. Hammond	v

V

Varlett, Judith	151, 157

W

Wadsworth, Joseph	117
Wakely, James	50
Wakeman, Sarah	43
Walcott, Mary	ix
Walkley, James	153, 157
Ward, Andrew	134
Ward, Hester	129, 136
Ward, Thomas	117
Webster, Mr.	38
Wells, Mr.	38, 129
Wells, Hugh	49
Wescot, Abigail	106, 112
Wescot, Daniel	101-116
White, John	38
Whiting, Rev. John	96, 97
Whitlock, Goodwife	134
Wiat, Nath.	102
Willard, Josiah	81
Williams, Abigail	ix

Williams, William	117
Willis, Samuel	78, 117
Wilson, Hannah	43
Wilton, David	51
Winthrop, John	35, 47, 143
Winthrop, Wait	27
Woodbridge, Rev. Timothy	76, 78
Woolcott, Mr.	38

Y

Young, Alse	35, 145-147, 156